BrandRituals

How Successful Brands Bond
with Customers for Life

ZAIN RAJ

spy glass
PUBLISHING

Mill Valley, CA

Published by
Spyglass Publishing Group, Inc.
100 Shoreline Highway
Mill Valley, CA 94941

Publisher's Cataloging-in-Publication Data
Raj, Zain.

> Brand rituals : how successful brands bond with customers for life / Zain Raj. – Mill Valley, CA : Spyglass Pub. Group Inc., 2012.

> p. ; cm.

> ISBN13: 978-0-9846337-0-8

> 1. Branding (Marketing). 2. Customer relations—Management. I. Title.

> HF5415.1255.R35 2012
> 658.827—dc22   2011919182

FIRST EDITION

Project coordination by Jenkins Group, Inc.
www.BookPublishing.com

Interior design by Shar Coulson
Interior layout by Brooke Camfield

Printed in the United States of America
16   15   14   13   12   •   5   4   3   2   1

Dedication

To Lubaina, my wife, for your love, encouragement and support.
To my children, Aamir and Sanaa, who make each day a pleasure.

Contents

Foreword: A NEW PATH TO SUCCESS   vii

1   Twentieth-Century Brand Wisdom   1

2   Twenty-First-Century Brand Realities   17

3   Enduring Myths and Misconceptions (LET GO OF THESE NOW)   35

4   The Power of Ritual   55

5   From Habits to Routines to Rituals: THE CUSTOMER DECIDES   75

6   Working the Intersections   87

7   Delivering a New Value Equation   103

8   Magnifying Consumer Attraction to Your Brand   121

9   Building Connections with Relevant Innovations and Experiences   137

10   Build a Bond by Aligning with Your Customer's Values   153

Afterword: ONLY THE BEGINNING   171

Recommended Reading/Further Reading   177

Acknowledgments   179

About the Author   180

Foreword
A NEW PATH TO SUCCESS

So you are now a vice president. You have climbed the ladder of success rung by painful rung until you've almost scaled the top. You have done beautifully. Unless you are vice president of [marketing]. In that case, you're in terrible trouble. There is one thing that can save you. You must get a brilliant idea. The best way to get a brilliant idea is to steal someone else's.

—*How to Succeed in Business without Really Trying*

When the movie *How to Succeed in Business without Really Trying* came out in 1967, marketing was just advertising. The wry description was that its job was to sell people things that they didn't really need for a price they couldn't really afford. And the job of the ad man was to come up with a campaign idea that would entice new customers to buy, buy, buy.

We shake our heads at the quaintness of it all. While many things have changed since then, two notable ones have not:

- As marketing professionals, we are still too obsessed with the idea of finding new customers—often to the detriment of existing ones.

- We are still looking for the brilliant idea that will save us.

This book has sprung from a combination of these two points (and a number of others we'll touch on soon).

This Book in One Paragraph

The marketing world must change because the consumer already has. And I'm not talking about the internet, digital and social media, or mobility. These are just channels to reach your target audiences. Consumers no longer wish to be sold anything. They are looking for products and services that offer a new definition of value, which doesn't necessarily include having the lowest price, and for companies that share their values. And to be successful in this environment, you can't just find the next new customer, and the next. You must create a bond with customers that actually changes their behavior and moves them from using your product occasionally to making it an integral part of their lives. That's what I mean by "brand ritual."

I think this is a brilliant idea worth stealing.

How This Book Works

I'm sorry: you can't succeed in marketing without really trying. But you can learn new ideas to help you direct that "trying" to areas that will move you further, faster. That's the underlying goal of this book. I've spent a lot of time researching, thinking about and trying strategies designed to get customers to behave the way we want them to. You'll find my road map here.

Chapters 1–3: Brand Basics

To know something, you have to *know* something. That's the function of these three chapters. They provide a basic understanding of the important ideas about branding and marketing and how both have evolved over the past fifty years. They also highlight important thoughts about today's consumer (including time starvation and the sound-bite society) and the marketing myths we can no longer afford to believe.

Chapters 4–6: Ritual Basics

I define "rituals" as the behaviors that spring from an integration of attitudes, beliefs, and behaviors. Here we examine the universal roles that rituals play in our lives and what gives them their power. Then we take a closer look at the progression of the behavior we want to instill in consumers, from habits to routines to rituals, and the frequency of use and modification of their beliefs required to get from one stage to the next.

Chapters 7–10: How Brand Rituals Get Built

There are points along the brand ritual continuum where customers decide how bonded they wish to be with a brand. I call these intersections. So we analyze what helps customers cross those intersections, as well as the key concepts of "mindfulness" and "engaging experiences."

Then we're off to the races with the four steps needed to create brand rituals:

1. *Getting the initial transaction*: Beginning with understanding the new value equation that determines how consumers define value today so you can get your foot in the door.

2. *Magnifying consumer attraction to your brand*: Including these characteristics: becoming digital at the core, inviting consumers into your brand, creating a value-added interaction, and delivering interest and relevancy.

3. *Building connections with relevant innovations and experiences*: Recognizing that this is the place where most companies stumble because they stay more focused on new customer acquisition and don't pay enough attention to existing customer needs.

4. *Creating a bond by aligning on key values*: The most sustainable bond is built when you can emotionally connect your customers with your brand by sharing the same kind of values.

Caution: many marketing professionals try to affect their customers at all of these stages at once. The only place that leads is failure. So examine your customer portfolio at each of these steps carefully and implement programs where they have the biggest potential for impact.

What Now?

I truly believe creating brand rituals is the best method for winning in the world of marketing today—and tomorrow. And I think this not just because these are my ideas, but 1) they are based on sound marketing constructs from some of the best minds in the business, which have stood the test of time and been updated to reflect what's happening today; and 2) I've used them for my clients, and they have worked.

So I invite you to read on and steal any brilliant ideas you find here—and accelerate your own success in the marketing business!

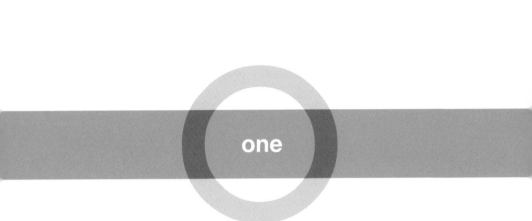

one

Twentieth-Century Brand Wisdom

Whatever happened to marketeers?

Not marketers—*marketeers*. The extra *e* is intentional, designed to change the very sound of the word so many of us have come to accept as a working professional title. People who go shopping, who take their cash and perceived needs to the marketplace, are marketers. They're going to market. People who try to understand customer attitudes and behavior so they can guide them in ways that benefit their companies are *marketeers*. They're the musketeers, the grenadiers, the bombardiers, on the corporate battlefield.

Or, at least, they should be.

But something has happened to marketeers in recent years. Take a look at an episode of the award-winning pop television hit *Mad Men*. It purports to take us back to a time when marketing was out on the cutting edge: hip, sexy, energetic, bold. That time was the early 1960s, half a century gone now, not the early years of the twenty-first century in which we live and work. Sure, it's television, so it's make-believe. But clearly, given its success, what's happening on the eye-catching retro re-creation of Madison Avenue that's home to the Sterling Cooper Draper Pryce advertising agency is a form of make-believe that's eminently believable to millions of viewers.

Then head west by northwest about 125 miles from Manhattan to the agency's modern-day fictional counterpart in beat-down Scranton, Pennsylvania, the dysfunctional enclave of the Dunder Mifflin Paper Company. Sales and marketing, as conducted through *The Office* there, is a decidedly lackluster endeavor. It's an endless tale of mediocrity rampant. Whatever talent some of its characters might once have exhibited is now stuck fast in the mud of petty politics, stifling bureaucracy, and feckless management. Again, it's make-believe—but, sadly, a form of make-believe that resonates with too many modern American workers.

Is the story arc of the field of brand-driven corporate marketing over the last fifty years all that different? Once upon a time, a time deeply embedded in the real-time memories of some of us still in the business today, marketeers had a seat at the head table. They—we—were wired in to the centers of corporate power, either directly or through the advertising agencies and marketing consulting firms. Companies relied upon us to help them build and expand competitive positions in the marketplace. Now, we're as often down a few floors from the rooms where the "big people" in the business hierarchy meet, relegated to support functions that seem to be running as much on their own momentum as due to any sense of intelligence and insight.

I'd like to suggest to you a surprising reason for that decline. Brands. Heretical as it sounds, I believe the fact that marketeers have lost their status and clout in the world of business today has a lot to do with how we've evolved our science of branding. Where once brand building was a key driver of business success, today brand management too often runs at cross purposes to both corporate realities and customer needs and desires.

It didn't have to turn out this way. And it doesn't have to continue to be this way. In fact, it can't. I contend that by understanding the dynamics of brand rituals, the phenomenon I'll describe here, within the context of the way we live and work and consume today, a new breed of marketeers can reassert its claim to a place at the head table. But it will mean letting go of some cherished myths and admitting that our world has changed, in many cases in ways we'll find challenging, even uncomfortable, in the years ahead. Doing so can position marketeers to help their organizations nurture lasting and profitable brand relationships with their mercurial customers. Failing to do so can only further marginalize our role in an ever-more-competitive business world—and ultimately threatens the long-term survival of the field itself.

Birth of the Brand

To understand how our present will define our future, it's worthwhile to take a less-than-rosy-hued look at our past: in particular, where the idea of branding originally came from and how it morphed into what it represents today. I'm not the first to attempt this analysis, and I surely won't be the last. In the last forty years, by my informal research, more than three thousand books have been written on brands and branding alone, and business books as a genre have grown from a small corner to several aisles in today's big-box bookstores.

Strangely, for all this history and growth—based on evidence both quantifiable and anecdotal (including what's on the tube at night)—we haven't become more effective when it comes to marketing. If anything, we've become less effective. Brand marketing messages have become ubiquitous and undifferentiated intrusions on the lives of our customers, integrated not only into ever-expanding time blocks in our mass media, but spammed into e-mail in-boxes, silk-screened onto shirts, tacked onto high-profile pieces of commercial real estate and entertainment events, inlaid into flooring, even posted above urinals. Yet research constantly finds that customers typically and consistently cannot name the last brand for which they saw or heard a marketing message.

There are any number of reasons for this disconnect, but let's start with a blinding flash of the obvious: cognition works. Customers learn from experience. They've had half a century to develop relationships with brands in our consumer-driven economy, where their economic activity represents fully 70 percent of GDP.

Consequently, brands are no longer mysteries to them. The in-depth and extended experience they've had with the brands woven into their daily lives gives them a behavioral lens through which to understand whether and how the brand delivers on the promises we've been making for it. This is far more than basic awareness, the goal of so much of our effort. It produces something I call "mindfulness": a generally clear and highly personal understanding of the role a brand plays in their lives.

Brands are no longer idealized concepts to our customers. They're part of the everyday world in which they live and work and consume. They see brands on real-world shelves, throughout the cluttered homes of their families and friends, in the bright sparkling newness of the bags they bring home from the store, and the battered used-up-ness of the remains they toss in the garbage.

Brands are not abstracts for today's consumers. They're real. Personal. Tactile. Malleable. What we say about our brands, the idealized image of them we try to conjure up in their minds, is only a part of what our customers know about them. They now have years—decades—of behavioral experience against which to weigh those words and images. As a result, they've learned to judge our claims and promises through their own personal filters. That's what builds loyalty, connectedness, mindfulness. It's also what encourages a growing resistance to many of our brand messages, as well as a willingness to modify those messages in ways they find personally meaningful.

Increasingly, our customers' growing knowledge of what we are saying and what they are doing with the brands we want them to choose and use empowers them to act in ways that were inconceivable even twenty years ago. As a result, businesses are finding that a lot of the basic tenets of mass marketing are being called into question, and in many cases are in clear need of modification. How we respond to this call for change—indeed, if we do this at all—is perhaps the key challenge facing us in the years to come.

A Unique Point of View

If you accept the premise that we live and work in an increasingly global economy—multicultural, multinational, multilingual—I bring a unique perspective to bear on this evolution. As you might have deduced from my name on the cover (or my picture on the back), I'm "not from around here" originally. I was born, reared, and educated in India, and not the India of modern technology manufacturing or outsourced service jobs. In the Bombay (now Mumbai) of my childhood, the water was turned on for an hour a day. Drinking, cooking, bathing: however much water your family needed for the coming day, you needed to get it right then or you did without. And in my neighborhood, we were considered relatively well off.

On November 1, 1984, I started my first job in marketing at InterPublicity, a small advertising agency in what is now the second largest city in the world. It's an easy date for me to remember because it was the day after the assassination of Indira Gandhi, India's trailblazing prime minister. I was so focused on making a good start on my first day at a new job that it never registered with me that everything in the nation was likely to be shut down. Despite curfews and widespread rumors of possible conflict, I showed up at the agency's office enthusiastic, energetic, and ready to work. It made a good first impression on my new boss. At least, I think she was impressed.

At InterPublicity, we functioned as a marketing partner and an extension of our clients' marketing departments. It was a very different style of marketing, however, because India at that time was a government-planned socialist economy, and had been since 1947. Marketing was not something that anybody thought much about, and advertising was not what most companies did. But all that was about to change. And I had a ringside seat.

In the aftermath of Mrs. Gandhi's assassination, her younger son, Rajiv, was nominated to take her place as the Indian National Congress Party's candidate for prime minister. He was elected in a landslide, helping the Congress Party amass the largest parliamentary majority in the country's history. Rajiv Gandhi had been a professional pilot before entering politics, so he'd seen the world. Educated abroad at Trinity College in Cambridge, England, and married to an Italian-born wife, he was very cosmopolitan. He'd had the opportunity to judge the strengths and weaknesses of those countries among which India aspired to take a place, and he knew things in his homeland had to change economically for that to happen. Over the next five years, he started an economic revolution that eventually transformed the nation, including opening up the entire socialistic marketplace to add some elements of capitalism.

Suddenly, there were new brands, new companies, new choices, new opportunities. The world of business began to change, and change rapidly. Literally overnight, marketing became an important discipline. But in the India of the mid-1980s, marketing was still at a fairly nascent stage. We were getting into the consumer brand-building game late, so we had a lot of catching up to do. In the U.S., the post–World War II consumer economy had been up and running for nearly four decades. Brands had been invented and positioned, had evolved and been reborn, often several times over, as the fabled rising tide raised all boats.

While we in India were trying to get up to speed on new concepts to address basic challenges, U.S.-based marketeers were into second and third generations of market and brand evolution. They had to be: during a quarter century of dizzying change, a small-town, close-to-home, nuclear-family-oriented nation had been transforming itself into an increasingly mobile, self-directed, and interconnected consumer-driven society.

From a commercial standpoint, the growth of familiar, dependable, national brands was a key component in this evolution. Shopping malls, for example. Over just thirty years of steady construction from their advent in the late 1950s through their saturation in the mid-1980s, indoor regional shopping malls transformed American retailing. They were big. They were clean. They were new. And they were responsible for drying up a lot of aging downtown commercial districts while laying the foundation for the counter-development, which began to arrive shortly thereafter: big-box stores, where customers didn't have to hike in from distant parking lots or walk by countless stores they weren't interested in to find the one place they wanted to go.

By 1984, while we in India were taking our first steps into this strange new world of modern consumer marketing,

- Apple, with a nod to George Orwell's searing vision, was releasing the Macintosh.

- Stonewashed jeans and rap music had debuted.

- MTV was three years old, and the first infomercials had begun appearing on U.S. television as cable channels proliferated and demanded something, anything, to fill their schedules.

- AT&T, after nearly ten years of antitrust conflict, had finally agreed to a court-ordered breakup.

- Post-it Notes already were in use worldwide.

And a number of names we still regard as "young" were already well along their growth curves. McDonald's, for example, was nearing its thirtieth birthday, with nearly eight thousand restaurants in thirty-two countries. Meanwhile, Walmart, though still primarily a small-town merchandiser operating in only half of U.S. states, was moving into its twenties, looking at major metropolitan areas for the growth Wall Street coveted and adding new formats like its first Sam's Clubs (named after founder Sam Walton).

Learning from Leaders

So, in Mumbai, starting virtually from scratch, we knew we had a lot of catching up to do. But we also had a lot of resources to draw on: a growing number of books were already available to help us understand, and leapfrog past, what had been learned in the more developed economies in the aftermath of World War II. If we could find them, that is. I remember going out to buy the latest marketing and advertising books that might have come in, including scrounging for copies at used bookstores. Whatever we found, we devoured, concentrating on the big picture and seeking out lessons learned half a world away that could help us make up for lost time.

There were a number of newly anointed legends on our bookshelves. *Reality in Advertising*, Rosser Reeves's trailblazing work, was the first marketing book I ever read. Philip Kotler's seminal book, *Marketing Management*, became a bible. David Ogilvy's books, *Confessions of an Advertising Man* and *Ogilvy on Advertising*, made this strange new business discipline real to us. Later, Bob Stone's book, *Successful Direct Marketing Methods*, was an indispensable guide as I developed the agency's first direct-marketing programs. And Al Ries and Jack Trout's breakthrough book, *Positioning: The Battle for Your Mind*, helped me understand how to lead on brand development.

When I say we were starting from scratch, I mean it literally. Sometimes we would memorize entire sections from one of these books, or others like them, then apply them without having any previous experiences or preconceived biases with which to modify the author's ideas. However, with forty years of recent business history outside of India to draw on, that actually had some significant benefits. We didn't have to learn our way through the basic steps and stages of creating a more consumer-sensitive economy. We could skip ahead to the more robust systems that were already proving themselves viable.

In India, to extend the earlier analogy, a strong new flood tide had started running before we had mastered many of the basics of brand seamanship. Consequently, our marketing efforts were an all-hands affair: everybody did everything because nobody had much experience at anything at that point. It was a tremendously stimulating learning environment, and it rewarded those who could do "integrated marketing" long before Don Schultz and Stan Tannenbaum made it fashionable in their book, *Integrated Marketing Communication.*

This was in marked contrast to what was developing in the U.S., where not only were different types of marketing businesses becoming discrete, but every discipline also was going through an evolution toward specialization. In India we did everything from advertising and direct marketing to trade shows and in-store displays. No detail was too small. It all connected to a larger, holistic effort. I remember supervising people as they painted local retail outlets with the new brand colors for the launch of Avanti mopeds. In the process, we learned to think holistically and agnostically, and to define every problem from a view that integrated business and marketing imperatives to build new brands while also growing the business.

My most defining experiences before coming to the U.S. were at Grey Advertising, which I joined in September 1985. Grey's agency in India was called Trikaya and was headed by a fantastic and legendary advertising professional named Ravi Gupta. During the late 1980s, he ran what was arguably the most creative agency in the country, even possibly South Asia. It was a place where new talent blossomed and new ways of marketing and thinking were developed.

Whatever the challenge, we took it on. High tech in the form of the first fax machines and the first size-to-size copiers for business. Durable goods, including luggage, two-wheeler mopeds, and tires for motor scooters. Entertainment, notably the debut of Nintendo Game Systems' iconic Super Mario Bros. As a consequence, I cut my marketing teeth on big-picture efforts that were free of the walls and silos beginning to divide U.S. marketing into segmented—and often jealously hostile—fiefdoms.

New Beginnings

What was true for us was equally true for our clients. If, as marketeers, we weren't very evolved in our understanding of marketing tactics, businesses in India were just learning their way around marketplaces where customers had choices, and the freedom and growing incomes with which to explore making them. Lacking extensive internal resources or experience, these organizations welcomed the broad-ranging expertise of our agency, and others like us, looking to us to be the X-factor that would help them develop a winning form of competitive differentiation. Because we were not specialized and segmented, we reinforced our much more holistic view of marketing's role in solving business problems.

When I came to the United States in 1990, I encountered a very different marketing world. In essence, I had to start my career all over again and learn a new, more specialized brand marketing model. (In case you're wondering why I made the move to Chicago, I met someone from "over here" at my brother's wedding. Three months later, while we were riding in a taxi through the busy streets of Mumbai, I proposed to her. She said yes and decided to bring me home with her. Best cab ride of my life.)

I started my career at Wunderman Cato Johnson, a pioneering direct-marketing and promotion agency. From there, I moved to Bayer Bess Vanderwarker (BBV), which was an independent general advertising agency that had a direct marketing arm called Kobs Gregory and Passavant (KGP). I was the person connecting the dots between BBV and KGP. After, among other things, developing the first loyalty program for dog food, I joined J. Walter Thompson in Chicago to run the Motorola cellular and infrastructure business on a global scale.

From there I landed at Foote, Cone & Belding, where I was part of the team that managed the SC Johnson Wax advertising account globally. Here I learned the discipline of developing strong and strategic brand propositions delivered through strong and effective advertising. SC Johnson would never run ads that did not deliver significantly above norm recall and persuasion. That level of discipline allowed them to build a portfolio of market-leading brands. In 1999, I followed the dot-com bubble to create and run FCB2.0, a digital branding practice. In the two years that we worked with a large number of dot-coms, I refined the disciplines of brand development and began to practice the principles that are espoused in this book.

During this period, I also began to see the cracks in the foundations of the basic rules of brand-building that had been in play since the 1960s. In those heady days, we were "building brands" in months. We saw businesses grow from infancy to global scale in a couple of years. We also saw consumers changing the way they defined their brand relationships.

When the dot-com boom turned to a bust, I was promoted to run FCBi Chicago, a direct, data, and digital agency (actually an aggregation of multiple agencies of FCB). At the time direct and data were more important than digital, which was still in its infancy. Here I was able to recognize how customer behavior was becoming more important and more sustainable in building brand preference than were customer attitudes alone toward the brands.

From FCB, after a stint as an entrepreneur, I landed up at Euro RSCG Worldwide, the world's fifth largest global agency network, where I spent six years helping to rebuild the Chicago agency and then creating and building a successful digital, data, and analytics company: Euro RSCG Discovery. I was also Global Practice Leader for Retail Brands. With Euro's roster of retail clients that included Tesco, Carrefour, Circuit City, and Homebase, to name a few, the intersection of behavior and attitudes provided some real-life lessons.

During this time at FCB and Euro RSCG, I was refining a new approach to building brands in this millennium, a process that led me in mid-2010 to accept the challenge of becoming President and COO of SolutionSet, the fourth largest independent behavioral marketing services company (digital, data, direct, and local marketing) in the U.S. Since then, I have been promoted to CEO and now have the joy and privilege of leading about 700 people across the country.

Along the way, I've had the chance to both observe and participate in the evolution of brand marketing, not only in the U.S. but worldwide. From the very beginning, I've been constantly conscious of the stark contrasts between the holistic and specialized perspectives that have defined my career. As the trail of agency descriptions above illustrates, with so much experience to build on, marketing in the U.S. economy had already grown large enough to begin fragmenting into specialized sub-disciplines, from traditional media advertising to targeted promotions and direct mail. As early as the late '80s and early '90s, that media growth and fragmentation, in turn, was inspiring new forms of marketing, from infomercials made possible by the FCC's deregulation of the airwaves to more targeted forms of placement as cable TV audiences self-segmented by specific interest. Since then, the same discussion has become rampant in the digital arena.

Seeing Forests *and* Trees

My background was as a generalist, but I quickly had to adjust to the reality that marketeers in the U.S. were already well along in their evolution to specialists. In the process, I saw them succumbing to the basic virus that invariably seems to infect any hierarchy: a fever for silo building. Each little subset of the marketing whole was busy staking out its own turf, evolving its own vernacular, competing for its own funding, and jealously (if blindly) guarding its own piece of the proverbial elephant.

There was notably little cross-pollination as this process gained momentum. The people who developed television commercials didn't interact much, if at all, with the people who put together direct-marketing programs. The direct marketeers had markedly different priorities and mindsets than those who developed and managed live events. The live events specialists didn't want anything to do with those who created online campaigns. The online folks were suspicious of efforts to launch loyalty marketing programs.

Unfortunately for marketing's long-term stature and access to the top, all the empire-building and turf-defending masked a more dire consequence: marketeers, whatever their subspecialty, didn't immediately notice that they were interacting less and less with the line-level executives who ran operating units and the top executives who were tasked with guiding ever-larger corporate conglomerations. In fact, "conglomeritis" was a term then much in vogue as mergers and acquisitions activities assembled odd collections of often unrelated businesses.

One result: brands started to become ends in themselves. When the name on the cover of the annual report had the potential to change, sometimes from year to year, the brand name provided the customer with a welcome consistency and continuity. For example, this year Parker Brothers, the makers of the classic board game Monopoly, might be owned by General Mills, the makers of Cheerios. That didn't matter to customers, whether shopping for family entertainment or breakfast cereal. Their relationship was with the brands, not the organizations that owned and managed them, however temporarily.

As the world of brands continued to develop and evolve, marketing's best and brightest were increasingly focusing on trying to create specific and accepting attitudes in customers' minds, often based on the specific brand, and not the real-world need or problem it was intended to meet. We became concerned with esoteric concepts like brand values and brand promises while looking for ways to position branded products and services in alignment with attitudes that we believed (or at least hoped) led to long-term loyalty. What did our customers aspire to? What made their eyeballs dilate and their palms sweat? And how could we connect with those emotional triggers?

In the real world of that era, the prime rate had recently touched 21 percent, the comparative quality of America's manufactured goods was looking quite shoddy, especially compared to the products coming across the Pacific from Japan, and Tom Peters was about to damn the emerging service economy in four memorably tart words: "Service in America stinks!" The operating managers that marketeers supposedly worked for were increasingly driven to demonstrate market mastery in basic dollars and cents.

Preoccupied more and more with the need to produce short-term results, line-level and higher execs alike began to tune out the branding cults in their own organizations. No matter: the various marketing fiefdoms within the organization and in agencies conceived and managed to support them stubbornly hunkered down behind their walls and promoted increasingly arcane measures of their success. Improvement in awareness, movement in attributes, likeability of the brand, and on and on and on—all attitudinal measures that did not directly relate to delivering meaningful and financially measurable customer transactions.

Birth of a Belief

Some twenty-five years later, nothing much has changed. In his 2008 book, *Branding Only Works on Cattle*, Jonathan Salem Baskin deconstructs one popular form of brand valuation, then pauses for effect:

> Gesundheit! Just revel in all that broad, ill-defined double-speak: *risk profile, considerations, market leadership, stability, global reach, ability to cross borders.* All these assessments and rates are qualitative estimates. This isn't math, it is religious scripture, created to reaffirm belief to the flock while ginning up enough obfuscation to dissuade nonbelievers.

Could HR or IT get away with trying to explain their expenditures with the language of branding, he wonders. No way: they'd get laughed at or fired—maybe both. To better see the contrasts between this fantasy world and business reality, Baskin suggests writing an actual sales number at the bottom of a piece of paper, then having someone who does branding for the organization diagram the process by which they get to that number.

"When you hit the first term or step that doesn't have a clear purpose or connection to that sales number on the bottom of your page," he advises, "look at the clock. My guesstimate is that it will take you under a minute to get there."

At moments like these, I go back to my roots, back to the contentions of the early influences in my career—Rosser Reeves, David Ogilvy, Bill Bernbach, Al Ries, Jack Trout, Phil Kotler, and others. Brand marketing, all brand marketing, must address customer needs in a differentiated manner to obtain sustainable transactions. The goal of the exercise is a behavior—buying something—not an attitude.

A customer who feels good about a brand but isn't buying it is of no immediate value. But, as we know, significant numbers of any given business's most loyal customers have attitudes that range from indifferent to outright hostile. Yet they continue to buy the brand, and frequently so, because it's an established behavior in their lives.

This is new ground. We've maintained for years that the key to making customers buy from us is making them like us. In our new time-starved, sound-bite-driven world, that's not necessarily the case. Welcome to the world of marketing in the age of brand agnosticism. Welcome to the age of brand rituals.

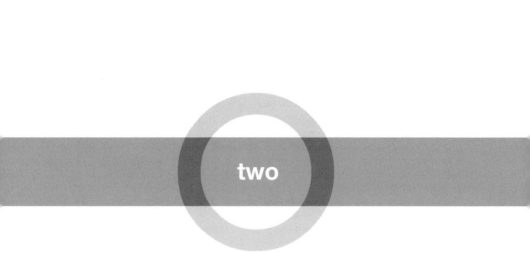

two

Twenty-First-Century Brand Realities

Fifty years ago, brands were the new reality.

They had existed prior to that time, to be sure. But not as a marketing preoccupation. In 1961, Rosser Reeves, purportedly the model for *Mad Men*'s Don Draper, wrote *Reality in Advertising,* one of the keystone books of modern marketing. In it, the man who pioneered television advertising in America at the Ted Bates Company introduced the concept of the Unique Selling Proposition (USP). He talked extensively about marketing's role in business, about measuring concepts such as penetration, usage, and pull. But he emphasized that advertising needs to contribute by making people behave a certain way: specifically, by buying something.

While Reeves didn't ignore the idea of brand image, which was just then coming into vogue, he clearly relegated it to a supporting role in the context of the Unique Selling Proposition. An engineer can indeed design a beautiful airplane, he conceded. But all that beauty will be pointless if the thing doesn't fly. Or, put another way, what you remember about a great speaker's dress and personality and emotions are brand image. What the orator said, on the other hand, is the Unique Selling Proposition. Given a choice between the feeling (brand image) and the claim (USP), "Surround the claim with the feeling," he advised.

In chapter 22 of *Reality in Advertising*, "The Law of Calculated Risk," Reeves offers—without citing a source for his figures or defining his criteria for success or failure—a stark comparison of results for big package-goods campaigns that "have flowed through our statistical mill." For 20 campaigns that emphasize Unique Selling Propositions:

10 good campaigns

6 excellent campaigns

2 brilliant campaigns

2 failures

"When we check on brand-image campaigns, however," he continues, "or the philosophy of feeling, these figures seem to reverse themselves. We find:

2 good campaigns

2 excellent campaigns

2 brilliant campaigns

14 failures

"In the reality of advertising," he concludes, "an agency's problem is not to write brand image. The problem, rather, is to *keep the creative people from writing brand image*—to insist that they think in those creative terms which may bring their clients the richest profits."[1]

Still Missing His Point

Think about the amount of business activity and brand growth worldwide in the 1960s and the decades to follow. Think about the emergence of the baby boom generation, the greatest brand-conscious customers ever set loose upon the planet. Think about the explosion of media worldwide, and the branded products and services whose advertising purchases would fuel its evolution in the years to come. And in one of the seminal books of the era, one of the smartest guys in the field of marketing consistently and emphatically subordinates brand issues to business priorities.

What he is talking about under the heading of a Unique Selling Proposition sounds almost quaint today. Even then, Reeves felt his provocative concept was often misunderstood. In *Reality in Advertising*, he specifies three key components, all of which were necessary as he defined the concept:

1. An advertisement must make a proposition to the consumer in which there is a specific benefit from making a purchase. Words and images are just so much window dressing unless they do this. In other words, the object of the exercise is to provoke action, not to create attitudes.

2. That proposition must indeed be unique, offering something the competition doesn't or can't.

3. And the proposition must be compelling enough to convince large numbers of customers to purchase the specific product or service in question.

By those criteria, a lot of the word salads promoted by businesses as Unique Selling Propositions today, some fifty years later, are neither unique nor demonstrably likely to result in sales. In a commoditized world, unique is often pretty hard to come by. And in markets with lots of lookalike offerings, it's typically hard to move the needle in large increments.

More to the point, what was a powerful new reality fifty years ago in turn has been eclipsed by the advent of two new realities: a world of time starvation and the advent in response of a Sound Bite Society.

The Value of Shortcuts

As we've already seen, the birth and steady expansion of the U.S. consumer-based economy in the years following World War II is one of the major financial stories of the modern era. And one of the key attributes of this phenomenon was the way the value of time changed, in the process bringing new forms of movement on a grand scale. Over the past half century:

- **People moved.** The American lifestyle sprawled out from central cities to expansive suburbs, transforming a decidedly stay-at-home form of life to one in which people were constantly on the go.

- **Families moved.** Promising opportunities might be down the street or across town, but they might as easily be halfway across the country. (Or halfway around the world.)

- **Generations moved.** All that movement segmented society by age. Once, several generations of a family could be found clustered around a hometown or region for decades. But since World War II, the nuclear family has fragmented, especially baby boomers' children, who have gone off to seek their fortunes essentially anywhere in the world, and without being restricted by geographic lines or time zones or family traditions.

- **Cities moved.** It was no longer necessary to live where you worked. The automobile became the indispensable key to turning time into advantageous movement.

- **Expectations moved.** A new American revolution was launched: the "revolution of rising expectations." Generations scarred by the depths of a Great Depression and the horrors of world war grew confident that their children would have more and live better. And they built an economy designed to provide just that.

- **Ideas moved.** Information no longer had to be gleaned from the written word in solitary concentration. Newspaper readership peaked and began a steady decline as radio, television, and mass entertainment brought more visual concepts to the fore. The internet and mobility has changed this to a whole new paradigm. Now we consume and distribute ideas and content in real time.

None of this movement would have been possible without the rapid exchange of information, from social opinions to laboratory research, that cross-pollinated ideas in a fraction of the time common in centuries past. In the popular culture, this first showed up in television, which, funded by brand advertising, rapidly evolved from a quirky curiosity set up in a corner of the living room to a colorful household appliance that became almost as ubiquitous and indispensable as table lamps.

In its own way, the tube turned the world into Marshall McLuhan's "global village." Anyone watching an entertainment program, a news report, or a commercial anywhere in the country, or eventually the world, became part of a community that transcended physical limits. In this new, open-bordered world, the time needed to communicate new ideas telescoped down from days to minutes, even as the sheer volume of messaging exploded. For their part, people linked electronically, regardless of their backgrounds or circumstances, and became united as "witnesses to history."

Then came the computer, that incredible shrinking thinking machine, and the pace of change went up another notch even as the scale of the technology imploded. From rooms full of lights and tubes designed only for big businesses and government agencies, ever smaller, more powerful, and more affordable machines became the common backbone for any number of smaller, more agile devices that could function, in the words of futurist Stan Davis, "any time, any place, no matter." With its connection to the internet, this device became indispensable "lifeware" for everything, from working and shopping to searching for information and staying in touch with family and friends.

Meanwhile, the simple telephone shook off decades of wearing basic black while being physically wired to the wall. Inspired by fast-evolving technology and freed-up competition, it grew at once more complex and more mobile, while becoming smaller and yet more powerful. In a suddenly wireless world, a once staid technology reached out to link people at home, at work, in public places, even in the car, in ways Alexander Graham Bell certainly never imagined.

Each technology broadened and accelerated communication, along with the pace of change. Each rewarded its users for the time they spent with it, but often at the expense of other demands on their time. Each encouraged its users to create their own form of shortcuts, from fast-forwarding prerecorded TV programming (in part to avoid being slowed down by commercials) to Googling high-profile events and unfamiliar concepts to (OMG) texting in a phonetically condensed argot. And watching their favorite shows on the go.

The Brandwagon Rolls On

All this time and motion continues to create new needs, and brands continue to answer many of them. In particular, they provide practical ways for people to maximize what they can accomplish with their limited time. When people lived and worked close to home, when their worlds were bounded by a box less than fifty miles a side, businesses were local and brands weren't that necessary. Mel's Barber Shop. Marty's Meat Market. Gayle's Bakery. Anita's Salon. Cliff's Repair Center. Kim's Café. Zain's Liquor Store. The scale and pace of life was compact enough to manage personally.

But today global trends reach from big cities to remote rural corners. Choices continue to expand as a result. Simply to make sense of them requires better tools for managing limited time and seemingly limitless space. We don't cook dinner these days so much as we assemble it. We don't spend a leisurely evening reading the newspaper; we surf the latest headlines from the time we get up in the morning until the time we shut down our electronic servants for the night. We don't spend time looking for a one-of-a-kind diamond in the local rough; we turn to the familiar brand name we've learned to depend on across zip codes and time zones.

Brands continue to make the challenges involved in time starvation at once more manageable and less time-intensive, less worrisome and more consistent. In a sense, they serve as informational shortcuts for a world in which the need to sift through reams of information faster and more effectively to find the essential nuggets shows no signs of abating.

If all this speed and motion is a little dizzying, a little disorientation is to be expected. It's easy to get caught up in the legacy of the many worthwhile results that have been produced by brand marketing through the last half century. Easy, but dangerous. Our world is constantly changing, and marketeers have to change with it. We can look at the way we've developed and understand why. But we shouldn't allow that to justify a sense of inertia, to stand pat and revere past practices simply because they worked once upon a time.

My point is that what worked in the past—a specialized approach to brand marketing that valued attitudes more than behaviors—is not going to work in the new world of limitless information and limited time and resources. The solution begins with regaining a more holistic understanding of marketing as a business resource, which means an emphasis on action: first, finding the right customers for an organization's products or services, and then motivating them not only to feel but to act in a certain way.

It's a challenge that will force us to explore new and more customer-centric solutions. The quickest way to see that is to look at the media we have relied on for decades now, where this evolution is already well-established. Once, the U.S. had three television networks, many large cities had multiple newspapers, and radio was a jumble of mostly local enterprises. It was an orderly world where information moved at a predictable pace.

Today the very concept of what constitutes an information and entertainment network is in flux, newspapers are fewer and slimmer, radio is heavily centralized, with national formats—and all three have been eclipsed by a dizzying variety of digital devices and technologies. As a result, information now spreads virally and with an immediacy that is at once amazing and appalling, especially for marketeers who believe they, and not customers, should ultimately control brand relationships.

Fragmentation is the rule, not the exception, and it's a pattern we should expect to be repeated in other places. Everybody knows it. Everybody talks about it. But we're still struggling to come to terms with what to do about it. Perhaps most notably, Al Ries and Jack Trout have pointed out some of the implications of living in what has become an "overcommunicated society."

Once, the idea of an Information Age was the stuff of futuristic rhapsody. Now, it's an often overwhelming reality. There's no dearth of information in our world today. We're drowning in the stuff. But if knowledge is power, it's modified in ways we're just beginning to understand.

Consider the mirror-image axioms that time is money and money is time. In a time-starved world, customers have less time to entertain our brand messages. But because cognition works, that's not a problem . . . for them. The time they've already invested in the brand relationships they value and find beneficial gives them a comfortable, functional way to accelerate their decision making while avoiding "wasting time" on other options.

The contrast is as stark as the challenge is troubling: while most businesses are still thinking in terms of thirty-second commercials and static imagery to engage their customers in time-intensive ways, a growing number of our customers—perhaps by now a majority—are time-shifting right by those carefully crafted and expensively placed brand messages to seek the specific ones that fit their immediate needs.

Changing Time Changes Everything

As we saw in the first chapter, while marketeers have devoted more and more attention to esoteric concepts that have less and less immediate impact on their businesses, larger forces have been changing the world we have to function in. The pace of life keeps speeding up. There is always more to do, more to know, and more to experience, but still only the same twenty-four hours in a day. To do more things, you have to spend less time on any one of them.

This is the new norm in our world, and you can see the effects all around us. People are working more and sleeping less. They make more purchase decisions but spend less time thinking about them.

They willingly forgo choice for convenience. Saving time, an oxymoron if ever there was one, has become a growing preoccupation. *Welcome to the era of Time Starvation.*

Many marketeers have noticed the symptoms, but few have understood the underlying causes. Think about reality then and reality today:

Then, families sat down to evening dinners that often involved half a day of food preparation by a stay-at-home housewife, leading to an hour or so at the table discussing the day, and often followed by another half an hour or more cleaning up. Now, both spouses likely work (if there are two adults in the household—half of all children in the U.S. at some point live in single-parent families), meals are catch-as-catch-can affairs, either assembled on the fly at home or consumed in a restaurant, and clean-up involves loading the dishwasher and tossing the wrappers.

Then, people had time to read for entertainment. Now, they park themselves in front of the tubes, which might be a TV screen, a computer monitor, or a handheld wireless device, and "time shift" only those pieces of programming that attract their interest (zapping past the commercials in the process). What's more, instead of viewing together as a family, they're often locked in on their own specific media, reflecting fragmented rather than socially unifying tastes. In 1960, people "consumed" five hours of media a day, according to a study conducted by the University of California, San Diego. Today, the average is twelve hours a day, and when people are online and watching TV at the same time, those hours count double.

Then, people had time to read for information. Now, they skim and sample and Google because their imperative is not to find out a lot about something "just in case" they ever need to know it; rather, it's to find out only enough about it to make a decision "just in time" to use it. In 2008, Americans consumed three times as much information each day as they did in 1960. Research by RescueTime, a maker of time-management tools, shows that the typical computer user visits forty websites on an average day, according to a *New York Times* report.

Starving for Time

Given the new urge to be productive virtually 24/7, and the sheer amount of time it takes, in the traditional sense, to be thorough in learning and understanding the crucial aspects of a potential decision, something's got to give. It has. Our attention span has not only fragmented, but the way we focus it also has changed in a significant way.

Increasingly, we make snap decisions. We do what's easiest and fastest at the moment, regardless of the long-term consequences. We rely on quick impressions, typically based on strong emotions—fear, anger, anxiety, elation, greed—rather than prolonged reasoning and a careful weighing of options.

It's not that there's no time. It's that every second seems to be filled to overflowing. In response, we learn to do what we have to do to cope. Let me offer a personal anecdote to illustrate what's involved.

Not long ago, I was driving my daughter to her voice lesson. She was twelve at that time. She has her own computer. She has her own e-mail account, which she checks faithfully. She has her own blog. She has a Facebook page with more than three hundred friends. She has her own iTouch, loaded with music, movies, and apps. She has her own Android phone with unlimited data and text plans. One recent month, she had 2,413 text messages. She also has all of the other time demands of a typical twelve-year-old: school, sports, friends, phone calls, parties, homework, books to read, chores to do.

As we were driving, she said, "Dad, right before we were going to leave, when you had me reading, you were just sitting in a chair in the family room, and you looked like you were in a daze. What was that about?" I replied that I hadn't been in a daze. I actually had been enjoying something I hadn't found time to do in a quite a while.

"What was that?" she wanted to know.

"Daydreaming."

You can imagine her response, right?

"What's daydreaming?"

At first, I thought she was teasing me. But, no, as it turned out, she really didn't know what daydreaming was. So, there in the car, I found myself trying to explain this, to me, familiar and pleasant use of time to my very bright twelve-year-old. It came out sounding like an attempt to bridge a new generation gap.

"Daydreaming," I said, "is something that I used to do a lot of when I was your age. I would sit, and I would close my eyes, and I would dream about things. I would dream about ideas. I would dream about things I would love to do. And that would inspire me. That would give me new ways of thinking. That would allow me to create innovations. That would allow me to think of something I wanted to do different from what I was. I don't have the time to do that anymore."

That's time starvation. When I was a child in India, my mother would often find me lying in bed in the middle of the afternoon, just dreaming about all the things I wanted to do. Now, not only am I not doing that, but my daughter can't even picture someone doing that. We've infected our children with our own form of overstimulation, filling every idle moment of their lives with sound and sensation and stuff to do right now, with no time for contemplation or reflection or just doing nothing . . . on purpose.

I take full responsibility for being a poor role model in this regard. As a member of the global economy, I am often on the phone at 10 p.m. and then back on the phone at 3 a.m. I'm answering e-mails 24/7. I'm working long hours, traveling constantly, always conscious of how much there is to do. As a result, when my daughter sees me not visibly doing something, it strikes her as so strange she has to ask me about it. And she has no frame of reference for my answer.

From Meaningful Meals to Bite-Sized

If Time Starvation is the disease, technology is the carrier. E-mails. Text messages. Phone calls. Computer collaboration. PDFs and PowerPoints and the proliferation of programming on TV and online, every minute of the day and night. Any message can be important. We can't risk ignoring any of them. There's no reliable way to prioritize, let alone wall off some quiet time for analysis and response.

So we look for ways to consume information that involve less time. Because of overcommunication, because of media fragmentation, because of intense time pressures, because of the half a century we have had to learn how to function in this economy and this world, we have become a Sound Bite Society.

(I won't claim to have coined this phrase. A gentleman named Jeffrey Scheuer wrote a book by that name a little more than ten years ago, originally published as *The Sound Bite Society: Television and the American Mind*. He focused on how television's basic communication style "helps the right and hurts the left," politically speaking, which is an argument for another book [and another audience]. I'm simply crediting him for coining a phrase that will be useful for our discussion.)

In the vernacular of modern media, a sound bite is a bite-sized chunk of content selected from a larger quotation. It's that brief moment when someone involved in the story being told on TV speaks about it, ideally in a pithy or emotionally engaging way. In television today, brevity might be the objective, but engagement is more likely the criterion for what gets on the air. In the famous description of Mark Twain, a good maxim provides "a minimum of sound to a maximum of sense." In our media-centric world, it's more like "a minimum of sound to a maximum of impact."

Generally, sound bites are used to provide the sound of someone's voice, after which the reporter or commentator explains the broader context for us. Students who analyze modern media in college classes often are amazed to find that the average sound bite we see and hear on the evening news lasts just ten to fifteen seconds, and many are shorter. How much can you really say in that amount of time? Not much! (Try it sometime. It'll make you very aware of just how little verbal content accompanies the pictures that give us our impressions of life around us.)

In a Sound Bite Society, we know intuitively that no one nugget of content can possibly provide enough information for us to make an informed choice. The trick, we learn, is to string together a succession of sound bites that, taken together, convey some sense of assurance that we have assembled enough of these bite-sized nuggets to make a good choice. Not necessarily the best choice. Perhaps not even the right choice. Just a choice that makes effective use of the time we can give to it.

It's like looking at a model railroading train table and picking out a succession of boxcars to link together into a train. We don't have time to look at every boxcar and consider whether it belongs in our train. We might wish we had time to duck under the table and get the red one over on the other side of the layout. But that's a lot of time to spend for one car, when we're trying to assemble something much larger. Odds are, we have to grab based on how much time we have right now, and how big we think our train is supposed to be, and which cars are closest and quickest to use.

Like so many boxcars being linked together piecemeal into a train, there's often no preset order for how the sound bites in our hypothetical train of thought and reasoning are selected and hooked up, let alone is there a sense that we need to have a certain number of them. As a result, for marketeers it's really terribly hard to anticipate which sound bites, and in which order, our customers will choose to rely on to make their decisions. And this evolution hasn't progressed toward anything near a new equilibrium, so our task isn't likely to get any easier anytime soon.

Small wonder there's so much clutter in our media, and our minds. Aided and abetted by digital technology that decentralizes information as it deconstructs and distributes it, the much ballyhooed Information Age has been turned on its ear. Once, we celebrated the growth of information and the increasing ease with which we could access it. Now, we're drowning in the stuff. And it all looks alike, which puts the onus on the consumer to judge which information is valid and which is hype. As marketeers have only begun to appreciate, any sense of message control is long gone, and with it much of the long-term retention of images and attitudes we spent fifty years learning how to create.

Seduced by Subjective Standards

As if the sheer glut of brand information available in our world weren't challenging enough, a second phenomenon has also begun to play a role. With so much stuff out there, and so little time to sift it, people are no longer processing information the way they used to. Once, they collected information, then studied it and tried to reach a conclusion justified by the range of facts at hand. Now, they simply try to string together a succession of sound bites to support the same conclusion.

Part of intelligence is relating unrelated things in a proper way. Many neuroscientists now believe we learn only by relating something new to something already known. My daughter didn't know what daydreaming was because she had never seen it before and had nothing to relate it to. Now that she has a reference point, she'll be better able to recognize the behavior if and when she encounters it again. Without similar contextual references, she won't be able to effectively judge whether she's seeing daydreaming or just directionless time-wasting. But with them she might be able to intuitively make the leap from an individual who's daydreaming to an artist who's pursuing a creative concept.

That brings up the idea of serendipity. Think about the absolute difference between poring through books and journals and other publications in a library and plugging a specific term into a search engine. In a publication, the information occurs in a logical sequence: you need to know this before you can understand that, and once you create that foundation, you can build up a more complex analysis. (That's how this book is organized, come to think of it.) In the process, you're typically exposed to a broader range of information than you were looking for, and that range often provides valuable context, if not for the immediate subject at hand then perhaps for something else you can't even anticipate at the moment.

A search engine returns only what you ask it for, ranked by its own peculiar algorithms that reflect anything but a logical progression. If the best (or at least most relevant) pieces of information, the key sound bites, don't turn up on the first couple of pages, how many people will ever find them? And does the seeker of sound bites have a frame of reference for telling the good information from the deliberately skewed, even incorrect, material that a search might return?

With the penetration of social media and adoption of social networks, information and connections come to us from different parts of the network without too many connection points. These create sound bites that we're now using to define our actions. It's different from how we've been conditioned in the past.

Solutions for a Sound Bite Society

What works now? What can marketeers trying to sift through the chaos of sound-bite saturation in a time-starved world turn to with some confidence that their desired messages have a chance to cut through the clutter and get through to their prime prospects?

- **Word of mouth.** If someone else has already assembled the sound bite train and customers have confidence that they know what they're doing, they're likely to decide that borrowing an established solution is much more time-efficient than creating a new one from scratch.

- **Time compressors.** Technology, the enabler of this evolution, has produced some notable responses to it, including social networking (Twitter might well be the classic model for the sound-bite economy); blogs run by users of a product or service, or sometimes its most vocal critics; and quick-search optimizers and services.

- **Personal experience.** As noted earlier, cognition works. People who make a judgment that's based on sound bites and find that it works out gain confidence in their ability to repeat the success. And they tend to tell their friends.

For marketeers, that creates some pressing challenges that call into question a lot of cherished assumptions, even as they promise workable solutions to the marketing challenges we face. Let's take a look at a few of the major ones to place the potential of brand rituals in their proper perspective.

Endnotes

1. Reeves, *Reality in Advertising*, pp. 84–85.

three

Enduring Myths and Misconceptions
(LET GO OF THESE NOW)

An oft-cited axiom called the First Rule of Holes counsels that when you're in one, you should stop digging. A German proverb asks, What's the good of running if you're on the wrong road? Ravi Gupta, my boss and mentor at Trikaya Grey back in Mumbai so many years ago, used to challenge me with a cryptic, "Look beyond the obvious, Zain," and liked to observe that "if there is no there there, there usually isn't"—which I eventually deciphered as meaning that just because something had been done before didn't mean it was the right thing to do again if it didn't make sense.

The immediate temptation when encountering new realities that promise to transform all the familiar rules and rituals we've found comfort in for so many years is to apply old solutions to them, whether or not they seem likely to work. After all, we've worked hard to learn these tactics through fifty years of brand development and management. Isn't it worth giving them yet one more try before we abandon them in search of something new—and undoubtedly different and uncomfortable?

Actually, no, it isn't.

We're entering new and largely uncharted territory in the way we identify, position, manage, and evolve brands. We'll do better in exploring this brave new world if we're focused on the challenges ahead of us rather than the baggage behind. In half a century of eventful growth and evolution, brands have built up their own mythology. Some of it's relevant, to be sure. But some of it is the twenty-first-century equivalent of flat-earth myopia. Once upon a time, people did indeed believe these things. And, to a certain extent, they had value in guiding our initial efforts in creating and building brands. (Flat-earthers might not have been in danger of sailing off the edge of the world, but staying within sight of land did keep a lot of them from being lost at sea.)

As with learning to circumnavigate the globe based on reliable astronomy, we have to be willing to leave behind the comforting sight of what we've known and venture forth into uncharted waters with a reliance on new ideas and instruments to guide us. There are discoveries to be made out there, and some of them will flabbergast us. There also are substantial risks among the rewards. The trick is to sail out boldly, with our attention focused on what's ahead of us, not distracted trying to find a way back to the familiar environs we've left behind.

Here are five basic myths we need to let go of if we're going to recognize brand rituals as the powerful force they can be in the years to come.

Myth #1: We Can and Should Change the Customer's Mind

When you look at the fundamental premises we have depended on in the marketing business over the past half century, the first one that leaps to prominence is the way we have focused on awareness and attitude almost as an end in itself, rather than as an enabler of behavior. In essence, we have built brands around the idea of moving things around in the customer's mind like so much mental furniture.

When customers were new to the idea of consuming, and both inexperienced and unsophisticated in the way they made purchase decisions, there was indeed a bankable form of value in building brand preference by first creating brand awareness. Before they could choose our potential solution over many equally unfamiliar others, customers had to know we could help them satisfy wants and needs they maybe never suspected they had. As they learned their way through the new consumer economies being created worldwide, it made sense that they should learn to feel confident and comfortable with our brand as the best choice for a given situation.

But one of the reasons marketeers have been excluded from operations-level decisions in recent years is the way we've turned this quest to drill down into the customer's brain matter into an arcane science that doesn't connect obviously or effectively to business needs and results. While the organization's key people have fixated on the measurable and manageable, we've shown a willingness to lose ourselves in fuzzy concepts and flashy creative campaigns that don't affect the financial realities of the business.

This is not to say that attitudinal concepts are wrong. In very valid ways, they have enabled the evolution of the marketing model itself. And there have been a number of noteworthy contributors in this regard:

- Al Ries and Jack Trout crystallized the whole concept of attitudes when they talked about owning a position on a ladder in the customer's mind. The best-known brand, the one that really stands for something, will be found on the top rung, they theorized. Rather than urge competitors to

climb up and displace a top brand from below, they coun-
seled essentially finding a new ladder where the top rung was
available and staking it out. The focus on brand leadership
was a good one. But they still concentrated mostly on playing around in the customer's mind rather than moving him
or her in the desired direction (toward the cash register).

- Ries and Trout are also deservedly well-known for their idea
of owning a word in the customer's mind. Making that one
word or phrase synonymous with the brand, like "safety"
for Volvo or "overnight" for FedEx, is a powerful idea. But
what makes that observation useful is the way those chosen
words connect with desirable customer behaviors. Car buy-
ers seeking safety actually do buy Volvos, just as customers
looking for reliable overnight service ship via FedEx. When
the word connects attitude to action, sales result. When it
doesn't, they don't. That's the essence of the exercise.

- In books like *Managing Brand Equity* and *Building Strong
Brands*, David Aaker talks about concepts like brand awareness and perceived quality, but again mostly in the context of
mind games, not behavioral actions. Yes, it can be useful to
align a brand personality with the characteristics of its target
customers—but only if they are moved to act on that affinity.

- Scott Bedbury, on the other hand, clearly has a behavioral
orientation. As the architect of Nike's classic "Just Do It"
campaign and the successful rebranding of Starbucks, the
author of *A New Brand World: Eight Principles for Achieving
Brand Leadership in the 21ˢᵗ Century* combines the traditional
marketing idea of owning a position in the customer's mind
with the current reality of making that position a keystone in
driving buying behavior.

That's obviously a small cross-section of a much wider and more diverse spectrum of thought and insight. But for years, some of the greatest thinkers in the brand space have focused on the same basic assumption: how we can change attitudes and expect behavior to follow? It's not a given that we can change the former, and it's even more uncertain that the latter will automatically follow. Nonetheless, as marketeers we've been encouraged to develop an almost religious attitude toward the principle.

That reverence might be appropriate in the context of rituals, I guess. But it's a dangerous precedent. In religion, people often are taught to revere the past so deeply and unquestioningly that they are forced to continue using ritualized ideas—which might well have made sense at one time—to dictate behavior in a new era, when they're not at all appropriate.

History has shown how that can lead to some very dysfunctional outcomes. Galileo spent some twenty years of his life under house arrest because the Catholic Church taught that the earth was the center of creation, and it didn't hold with folks like Copernicus using that newfangled science stuff to prove otherwise. A contemporary of Galileo, Jordano Bruno, was even burned as a heretic by the Inquisition for not repenting of this scientific sacrilege. Yet for all the fervor the witch-burners brought to the pyre, today their behavior looks dumb because the set of things "everybody knows" has changed.

Aside: This wasn't "new" news: Egyptian astrologers some 2,500 years ago had calculated that the earth was round and in orbit around the sun, not vice versa, based on observing, and then painstakingly measuring, the variation in shadows cast down wells near their desert monasteries. They had, as I recall, even come up with a figure for the circumference of the earth that was within a few thousand miles of what we would "discover" a couple thousand years later.

The key point is that when conditions change, our thinking has to change accordingly. And the sooner the better. What worked in the past undeniably did work. At that time. But that doesn't mean it will always work, especially when underlying conditions are in so much flux. As the new realities of marketing have permeated our world, our thinking has been slow to keep pace. Too often, we still rely on brand *images* and *attitudes* that we try to create in the space between the customer's ears, rather than brand *behaviors* that take place in the real-world space where products are consumed and services selected.

It's time then to shed light again on the fundamental principles around brand marketing. Way back in 1927, Albert Lasker, who founded the firm I would later work for as Foote, Cone & Belding, went on record as saying, "Advertising is salesmanship in print." The role for any marketing effort, he contended, should be to sell: to get the desired behavior, not simply a desirable attitude.

As previously discussed, Rosser Reeves was another behavioral believer: his Unique Selling Proposition was all about creating pull and expanding usage. Similarly, David Ogilvy, even though he is credited for being one of the creative advocates of modern brand advertising, clearly believed that advertising and marketing should sell products for his clients. He believed that a good advertisement is one that sells the product without drawing attention to itself. And that if it doesn't sell, it isn't creative. He also believed that in the modern world of business, it is useless to be a creative, original thinker unless you can also sell what you create.

At the end of the day, simply trying to fill people's heads with stuff, no matter how capably crafted or cogently reasoned, is no longer enough. In a business world where survival is an increasingly pressing issue, if the long-term concepts we're trying to insert into customers' minds don't lead to short-term action, we've essentially wasted a significant amount of the energy and company treasure that we spent creating and spreading them. On the other hand, pioneers like Ogilvy, Reeves, and Lasker all believed that successful marketing and advertising programs had one main goal: to build strong brands by building sales.

Like these enduring leaders for our field, behavioral scientists today focus not on thought but action. It's not about what someone thinks or understands or believes. It's about what they do. Unless thought leads to action, unless attitudes inform and direct behaviors, it's not real, no matter how pretty it might be. And it's not going to build sustainable and profitable brands moving forward. The only brand truth at the end of the day is what we do that actually makes the cash register ring.

Myth #2: We Can Assume the Customer Is Interested

No, we can't. Not anymore. At least not on a large scale. In a world where we are overcommitted, overextended, and stretched beyond our limits—time-starved, when decisions are made on the spur of the moment by assembling sound bites rather than by deliberately acquiring information and weighing various options over time—it's not a given that customers even know which brands they're purchasing on a regular basis.

They've been buying ketchup and motor oil and golf shirts and alkaline batteries for years now. In their minds, these products, and a bucketful of services as well, have become commodities. They basically look alike. They basically operate alike. So if they aren't priced alike, customers understandably start to question paying more for this one than that one.

This is a fundamental reason why private-label brands continue to grow their share, not only on retail shelves but also in consumers' pantries. According to the January/February 2010 issue of *Private Label Magazine*, store brands in U.S. supermarkets reached an unprecedented 23 percent market share in 2009. Total sales of store brands surpassed $85 billion as the industry recorded annual sales gains between 6 and 10 percent in supermarkets, drug stores, and mass merchandisers.

"Rather than a temporary effect of uncertain economic times," the magazine noted, "there are clear indications that retailers are winning new supporters to their brands."

There's also a phenomenon called *plateauing*. When something new comes along, like computers or cordless phones or laparoscopic surgery, there's an initial period of adjustment as customers learn how to make the best use of the new offering. But in relatively little time, they achieve a basic familiarity and find they know what they need to know to make whatever it is do what they need it to do.

Fifty years ago, test driving a car was very important to buying one. Cars were improving. Roads were spreading. Lifestyles were expanding. Brands were growing. Millions of new drivers, and even lots of experienced ones, needed to become familiar with the new performance capabilities being offered to them, so a test drive was an important aspect of their purchase process. With very few exceptions, that's no longer the case today. Imagine someone who's been in a coma since 1970 coming out of it this morning. If they wandered outside and got behind the wheel of a car, they might have trouble figuring out the GPS and multifunction stereo built into the dash. But they'd be justifiably confident that they could master the process of putting the key in the ignition, put the car in gear, and figure out which foot pedal makes the car go faster and which one slows it down.

Consequently, test drives today are more a matter of occupying customers for extended periods of time, which effectively reduces their already scarce time for comparison shopping. Knowing this, some car dealers train their salespeople to literally try to keep customers on the lot for a targeted period of time: an hour, ninety minutes, even two hours. In some cases, the intent almost seems to be to create a form of Stockholm Syndrome, the phenomenon in which hostages come to identify with their captors. It's as if the longer the sales staff can keep us captive on the lot, the better the odds they'll break us down and get us to buy their offering—if only so we can get away.

I think a lot of people who create brands start from the premise that they've come up with something new and cool and never before encountered, which makes it imperative that they grab customers by the lapels and regale them with the full spectrum of features, advantages, and benefits they've built into whatever it is they're trying to sell. In actuality, there are precious few people in the world walking around thinking, "Oh me, oh my, I want something to come into my life tomorrow, an exciting new product or service, that will change my life." Who has that kind of time? As marketeers, we are constantly out there saying "new" and "improved," confident in the underlying assumption that customers are waiting expectantly for that change and will willingly invest their time in understanding the tiny incremental differences involved.

They're not. They won't.

In some respects, this connects to the build-a-better-mousetrap mythology: the belief that the marketplace invariably rewards innovation. In some things it does and has, but only to a point. When either (a) you hit a sufficient quality level that the supposed innovation is largely incremental or (b) the customer doesn't have the ability or willingness to pay more for something, even if it does indeed do more for them, the supposed better mousetrap doesn't become a mass phenomenon.

In our currently maturing economy, customers have limits on what they can buy these days. Their incomes aren't growing. Their credit cards are maxed. Their home equity has been bled away by the collapse of housing values. Their 401(k) took a hit in the market meltdown. They have to be smarter about what they buy. Brands can play a role in that, but often more as a function of rituals that develop around something known rather than explorations of things that promise to be new and different.

The iPad, for example, is a phenomenon—possibly a mass phenomenon. Even though relatively few people were drawn to it initially,

Apple laid the foundation for a transformational success story based on form and function, not hype. As it becomes more popular, its price point drops (a predictable development, based on economies of scale), and as the arrival of competing Android and Windows 7 platforms and devices enriches the field, this market will grow. To what extent? I believe it will replace the laptop computer by doing the things that a bulkier, more expensive, and less user-friendly generation of machines has been doing, but doing them smaller, better, faster, and cheaper.

Myth #3: The Key to Building Brands Is Advertising

Brands are not something marketeers create out of thin air. In reality, a brand is only valuable—in essence, it only becomes a brand—when customers decide it has a reason for being a part of their lives. The consumer's experience creates and validates the brand, not marketeers or advertising. The Gap learned that lesson, to its highly visible chagrin, in 2010 when it rolled out a new logo, only to have it roll it right back up just a week later and return to its old familiar one when the online community erupted in howls of criticism. In 2009, Tropicana got its brand nose bloodied in similar circumstances, rolling out a package redesign its customers plainly did not want or welcome. By the time it had restored what its customers wanted, estimates suggest the company had wasted hundreds of millions of dollars.

A few years ago, we saw the functional emptiness of the myth of advertising as brand catalyst repeatedly demonstrated during the Super Bowl. A number of new "brands" appeared whose primary value promise seemed to be that they must be important and worthwhile—and real—because their creators were advertising them in this highest of high-profile football games.

In a way, their creators fell victim to a distortion of the Super Bowl's own brand identity: although ostensibly it is the championship game that ends, with great flourish and fanfare, the National Football League's season, in recent years people seem to pay more attention to the commercials than the game itself. And each year, it seems, this mythology grows. Genial TV newsreaders from Manhattan, New York, to Manhattan, Kansas, to Manhattan Beach, California, profoundly discuss the game's best and worst ads. Magazines and newspapers run advance previews and post-game compilations. Our industry's trade media provide learned analysis on the techniques used and rapturous commentary on the stories behind the little mini-dramas.

Does customer behavior change? With very few exceptions, no, it doesn't. Remember Go Daddy's provocative and much-discussed ads on Super Bowls from 2005 on? The ads often were the most talked about commercials from their respective games and created a lot of buzz for their "Go Daddy Girls," including NASCAR driver Danica Patrick. But Go Daddy withdrew a 2006 IPO due to market uncertainties, and each year, after the initial postgame buzz had passed, the company continued struggling to differentiate its business model.

Similarly, CareerBuilder.com, an online employment website, put together a string of memorable and entertaining Super Bowl ads featuring long-suffering human protagonists working amid the antics of dressed-for-success chimps in the workplace. People loved the ads, but the needle on business revenue didn't move enough to justify the investment.

The idea that, in today's commoditized environment, brands get built by advertising is a huge myth. You can create a wonderful commercial. You can put it on the Super Bowl. You can spend millions of dollars providing hundreds of repeat impressions to millions of customers and tell yourself it's all worthwhile because people now know your brand's name. But it's an absolute waste if, at the end of the day, people aren't using the product or service, figuring out the role it can play in their lives, and deciding to use it again.

Many years ago, I had the great good fortune to work with Bill Perez when he was the CEO of SC Johnson. He went on to become CEO of Nike and Wrigley, but I knew him back in the days when he led a classic and successful consumer packaged goods company. In those days, an accepted axiom was that you could get growth or you could get profits, but you couldn't get both: the cost of driving growth would detract from profitability. You had to invest (spend revenue) now to earn profits later, the brand gurus insisted. Bill Perez didn't buy that. "I want to drive *profitable* growth," he would insist.

As marketeers steeped in the clan secrets of our trade, we tried to tell him competitors were spending more than he was on advertising, and he needed to invest more in advertising to strengthen his brand equity. He looked at us like we were from Mars. "I have over 50 percent share in most of my categories," I can still remember him telling us. "That means over half the people out there are buying my brands right now and using them. That means I have strong brand equity."

For me, that became a fundamental ah-ha moment because it drove home the salient point that it really doesn't matter what people are *thinking* about a brand. It matters what people are *doing* with a brand. Marketing research might indeed find people who say they love the brand, they trust the brand, they think highly of the brand, they respect the brand. But do they buy the brand? Do they use it? Over and over again? When more than 50 percent of the market consistently chooses your products or services, you know you have a strong brand.

Today, this principle has even more relevance because as we constantly look for new ways to get brand messages in front of customers (California is actually looking at adopting electronic license plates that could carry sponsor messages . . . in traffic!), customers are looking for ways to avoid our messages as much as possible. They routinely time-shift their favorite programs, for example, recording them for later viewing (even if "later" is as little as fifteen minutes after the program starts) so they can zap past the commercials and just watch the show. Or they tune in online and skip the commercials entirely.

Are your ad campaigns still built on the familiar thirty-second spot? If your customers' remotes can advance recorded programs in one-minute increments, it's very possible they're receiving absolutely no exposure to your message. They literally don't know what they're missing.

Smart marketeers are addressing this issue. We are beginning to develop commercials and other ads that deliver on core needs and insights. New IP-based technologies are allowing us to make these ads relevant by households. New formats—long-form commercials, multi-page books, view-on-demand—and other technology-driven advances are allowing us to address consumer needs with measurably more relevant messaging.

Myth #4: The New Key to Building Brands Is Social Media

Unless you've been living and working in a cave, you know the advent and continuing growth of social media has transformed communications. It doesn't follow that it will transform marketing.

My reasoning for saying this shouldn't be surprising by this point: The issue is not about what this new wrinkle can do to further extend brand communications. It's about what it represents for the entire business and whether incorporating social media into the mix makes sense for the organization and its various brands.

In a way, I'm a confirmed "rational pragmatist" on the subject of social media and have been for some time. In early 2009, for example, Reuters interviewed me for a piece on social media in retail marketing. Everybody else the reporter talked to echoed the same refrain:

"Every marketeer needs to be in social media." "We can't afford not to be in there." "This changes everything."

My response: "That's crazy."

Yes, we need to have a social media *strategy*. But before we commit valuable resources to social media *tactics*, the strategy needs to help us understand the challenges we have to address and the operating models we have to examine so we're seeing social media's potential as not just another marketing channel but a way to address real business imperatives. Otherwise, we're doing the same thing that those well-intentioned marketeers did in focusing on Super Bowl ads for brands that had no business advertising on the big game.

It's an apt comparison. The sheer weight of activity that has rapidly developed around the Facebooks and the Twitters and the Flickrs and whatever other new forms of social media have popped up since this passage was written can easily seduce us into believing we have to get in this game simply because everybody else is.

But there's also a waggish saying sometimes referred to as the First Rule of Technology: just because you *can* do something doesn't mean you *should*. Yes, you can make a mechanical bass that hangs on the wall and sings an obnoxious song at anyone who trips its motion detector. But why? Marketeers would be well-advised to keep this principle in mind as they evaluate what role social media should play in their brand marketing activities.

The promise of social media can indeed be valid: providing a broader and deeper brand experience. The temptation is to jump in with both feet and commit all hands to getting social media efforts up and running, whatever their nature or business justification. The blind spot is, once again, whether this is something the customer wants and values. For all its sudden rise to prominence, social media is one more channel for communicating brand messages and interacting with customers. And a growing number of researchers and commentators are noticing some pushback as users begin to add up the sheer amount of time they're spending with these tools. Remember all that discussion about time starvation? Anything that eats time in our busy world without commensurate value has the potential to hinder as well as help.

What is significantly different about social media as a channel is that, much like a retail store setting, it allows a business to interact with its customers in meaningful ways. That's potentially terrific in the sense that we can open up a channel that provides on-point, unfiltered information into the relationship between customer attitudes and customer behaviors, and valuable new information flows among the customers and employees and stakeholders of the business. But it's also potentially dangerous in the sense that having opened up this channel, it now becomes incumbent on us to manage what's going on in it promptly and effectively. When you invite customers to tell you something about your brands, you have to accept and react to what they tell you. And, given that we're talking electronic media here, you have to do so in real time, regardless of how well your systems and people are prepared to do that.

Consider the saga of Canadian Dave Carroll and his beloved $3,500 Taylor guitar. In mid-2008, he was on a United Airlines flight through O'Hare in Chicago only to see his cased guitar and other instruments from his band being thrown around by baggage handlers while his flight waited near the gate. It cost him $1,200 to get the Taylor repaired, but when he filed a damage claim with the airline, it was rejected. End of story, right? Not in the internet age.

After months of frustrating negotiations with United went nowhere, Carroll went online, promising to post not just one, but three videos of songs he would write and perform lamenting what happened to his favorite instrument. Within days of its release, the original, "United Breaks Guitars," had been viewed on YouTube more than three million times (the total was nearing eleven million by August 2011), and Carroll became the poster child for aggrieved customers everywhere.

Some online commentators still attribute a 10 percent drop in United's stock price a few days after the first song went online to the resulting public furor, but lower quarterly earnings were a more likely reason, and the stock price soon recovered. More to the point, the legend lives on years after the fact (especially among musicians) and provides eloquent evidence of the power of viral information in a wired world.

For stonewalling a claim that amounted to pocket change, a major corporation found itself spending uncalculated hours (and dollars) answering countless media inquiries, responding to fliers worldwide who professed to be everything from sympathetic to outraged, and defending its reputation and employees from people who heard various versions of the story long after the fact.

And what might United have accomplished in earning customer and public goodwill instead of virtual brickbats by simply providing the $1,200 in vouchers Carroll asked for to offset the money he spent on repairs when the issue first came up? Stung by the online whirlwind, the airline eventually did offer to compensate the guitarist, but seven months after the fact. Carroll turned them down. He decided he'd rather make a point and provide an object lesson in what can happen when a big system runs over a small but web-savvy individual. He did.

The moral of the story: being active in social media should not be a marketing decision. It needs to be a business decision, and it needs to resonate with business values, including timely and effective communication. It also needs to serve valid business purposes, and in ways that anticipate both the advantages and the jeopardies of this medium.

A brand doesn't belong to marketing. A brand belongs to the customer. The customer doesn't belong to marketing. The customer belongs to the business. It's a very simple premise to state, but a very difficult one to manage effectively.

Myth #5: Acquiring New Customers Is Always the Top Priority

In the high-growth years of the consumer economy that grew up worldwide in the aftermath of World War II, businesses focused on growth. In most cases, the easiest way to achieve that growth was a function of three kinds of more: more customers with more money who buy more stuff.

- If you could expand the spectrum of customers attracted to your brand, your business grew.

- If you could entice your customers to pay a higher price for what you offered, whether directly by increasing what you charged them or indirectly by being more efficient about managing the costs of design, production, marketing, and sales, your business grew.

- And if you could expand the range of offerings you brought to the marketplace, selling to existing as well as to new customers something they weren't already buying from you, your business grew.

Small wonder that we got in the habit of focusing on the chase: putting our best minds and most creative campaigners to work on bringing in new customers. But in the process, we tended to overlook the reality of what has now become significant enough to gain its own acronym: CRM. Customer Relationship Management. So what if we were losing 5 percent, 7 percent, even 10 percent of our base every year? In a high-growth world, we were growing that base by 20, or 30, or 40 percent or more. No matter how much we spilled, it was so much easier to simply work that much harder to replace them.

No more. In today's saturated marketplaces, the best customer to have is the one you've already got. Existing customers know your brand. They buy your brand. They're predisposed to come back and do business with you again—that is, if you don't make it so hard for them or so obnoxious for them that you make other alternatives more attractive. Today, some of the best marketeers, some of the best businesses, have learned to do a much better job of actually managing existing customers. They focus on drawing out the value and deepening the loyalty of existing customers, including stopping attrition, before they pursue new ones.

The fundamental math is inescapable. If you lose a customer, especially a good customer, it will take a new customer at least four to five years to generate as much profitable value. Your existing customers know their way around your business, both in the physical and the virtual sense. They're comfortable with your systems. They understand your pricing. They have come to accept, and outright trust, the underlying quality of what you're offering them. A new customer has to learn all of this and more.

Take retail as an example. When you walk into a retail store for the first time, you're likely to be what marketeers call a "mission shopper." You're there to buy something, and, given the realities of time starvation, you're on a mission to find it as quickly and effortlessly as possible. You get in, you ask someone where to find what you want, you go there, you get it, you pay for it, you get out. The next time you go there, you have a sense of familiarity that allows you to relax and explore a little more. What else does this place have, you wonder. What else can it do for me?

Tesco, the United Kingdom's No. 1 retailer and the world's most successful internet supermarket definitely understands this principle. As Terry Hunt, who helped steer the development, launch, and continuing creative strategy for the Tesco Clubcard—widely considered the world's most successful retail loyalty program—explains, "You don't really know what behavioral change is genuinely important until you see it in action, on scale."

And that leads to behavioral results that can be measured. Tesco's program, which debuted in 1995 and in its fifteenth year had some eleven million members, generates more than £100 million in incremental sales every year while also earning profits every year. And it does so by emphasizing customers Tesco has already acquired.

"Small changes of behaviours, achieved across the entire customer base of millions of households, add up to a considerable boost in sales and profitability for Tesco," say the authors in *Scoring Points: How Tesco Continues to Win Customer Loyalty.* "Customers may not even perceive that their spending at Tesco has increased. But in general they definitely feel that they are rewarded for being a customer, and recognized and appreciated as a good customer. A loyalty programme does not change their life, it does not keep them awake at night in anticipation, but it does give them a reason to prefer the brand."

The Role of Rituals

This is where brand rituals begin to enter the picture. If you're feeling time-starved, a routine you already know and can easily repeat is much more time-effective than feeling your way through a new Skinner Box of steps and stages. If you're reduced to relying on sound bites to make decisions, the fastest way to solve for x is the way you've done it before. If you're a little insecure from all the speed and turmoil and trauma of modern life, there's comfort to be found in rewarded practices that place you on an island of familiarity amidst a sea of change.

With this in mind, it's time to dig a little deeper into the values and the complexities of rituals in general.

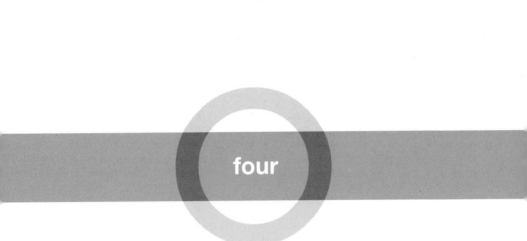

four

The Power of Ritual

In the first three chapters, we looked at the concept of branding: Where it came from. How it evolved, particularly in the U.S. in the years after World War II. What it has come to represent in modern business worldwide. And how we, as marketeers, have become marginalized as the science of our art has become increasingly oriented toward attitudes rather than behaviors. While we've been focusing our creative energies on what customers think and feel about our brands, the world of business itself has become increasingly conscious of the hard reality that it's what customers *do* with them that matters—specifically, what they buy and don't buy.

Originally, that was central to our belief as well: Rosser Reeves, one of the founding figures of modern marketing, was prominent among those who believed the basic purpose of marketing efforts was to move the needle on sales in meaningful and measurable ways. And right away.

As he said in *Reality in Advertising* about his seminal Unique Selling Proposition (USP) approach, "It formulates certain theories of advertising, many quite new, and all based on 20 years of intensive research. These theories, whose value has been proven in the marketplace, revolve around the central concept that success in selling a product is the key criterion of advertising."

As we've seen, clearly there can be links between attitude and behavior. In the early years of consumer-driven economies, as customers learned their way into important new roles as the drivers of business activity, it made sense for marketeers to better understand what goes on in customers' minds to better draw them to the choices we wanted them to make. In a still-formative consumer world, where customers were largely unaware of the choices available to them and had relatively little experience with turning those choices into longer-term behaviors, this made sense.

But as we've also seen, customers learn from experience. Cognition works. Today's savvy baby boomers have better than sixty years of experience being consumers. Every choice they've made for decades now has empowered a bedrock belief in their ability to decide for themselves what and when and why to buy. What's more, their children have grown up with the expectation that anything they want will be readily available to them. And virtually any choice they make will be good enough.

Consequently, our world has changed, even if we haven't noticed. What once could be a somewhat long and involved thought process leading to a purchase decision, where marketeers played an important role in shaping attitudes that led to buying behaviors, has steadily winnowed into a quick form of action and reaction that often involves very little conscious thought on the customer's part. At the same time, customers know from their own experiences that they don't have to like a choice to make a choice. Attitude, schmattitude: just give me what I want right now and I'll be on my way.

Contributing to this behavioral evolution is the nature of our world itself: fast-paced and characterized by constant change, where decisions increasingly are based on short chains of sound bites rather than deep and time-devouring research and deliberation. In trying to make the best use of our choices in this time-starved, multitasking environment, Nike's enduring bite-sized slogan rules: just do it.

Changing economic conditions will likely play an increasingly important role in the relationships between brands and customers, one I think marketeers will spend a great deal of time wrestling with in the years to come. We come from a tradition of abundance: in the early years of the consumer economy, as incomes rose, choices expanded, quality improved, and prices stabilized with scale and efficiency, the rule of thumb was essentially, "If you want it, chances are you can have it."

We don't live in that world anymore, and just as the Great Depression of the 1930s scarred the generations that went through it, what has happened in our world in recent years is undoubtedly going to leave a scar. While we still have choices in abundance, making them runs up against a variety of adverse factors: stagnant wages, reduced employment and advancement opportunities, imploded housing values, diminished savings and retirement programs, tighter consumer credit, and restricted public-sector support. Regardless of what they might want, customers' ability to buy anything at all is not a given in the years immediately ahead.

At first glance, it might therefore seem strange to nominate ritual as a potential solution to a marketeer's dilemma. Aren't rituals themselves also attitudinal in nature, anchored in thoughts and feelings and deep-seated mental constructs? Aren't they less stable and lasting than in decades past, more prone to doubt and change in a skeptical world where knowledge often circulates in random and unpredictable ways?

To some extent, yes on both counts. But the salient point here is that rituals, whatever the attitudes that underlie them, are behaviors.

And that's the objective for our analysis: understanding bankable behaviors that elevate brand relationships to the level of brand-bonded actions.

Common Threads, Uncommon Garments

Rituals have been with us for thousands of years. What's more, they're remarkably consistent across different cultures and eras. The attitudes they're based on can be very different. Yet the behaviors through which they are expressed generally turn out to be very similar.

Because I'm from India, I have context for my understanding of ritual that might be unfamiliar to you. It's Mohenjo Daro, an ancient city on the Indian subcontinent whose civilization predates ours by some four thousand years. Much like that age's Babylonians and the Egyptian civilizations of pyramids and sphinxes, the civilization that built Mohenjo Daro grew to regional prominence, flourished for centuries, and then unaccountably vanished, leaving behind ruins and runes that we can only speculate about today.

Mohenjo Daro, "mound of the dead" in the ancient Sindhi language, was an administrative center that rose in the Indus Valley. Between 2600 and 1900 BCE, the Indus Valley Civilization—considered one of the world's first great civilizations—dominated a region that includes what is today northern India and Pakistan, with outposts as far west as Iran and as far north as Bactria. Archaeologists think this vigorous and prosperous society might have had a population of more than five million people at its peak.

Mohenjo Daro apparently was one of its key centers, a well-planned city nearly a square mile in size along the Indus River, with more than thirty thousand residents. It was both well-designed and well-administered. Its streets were laid out on a grid. There were public baths, and most homes were connected to a covered wastewater system that helped keep the city clean and make good use of a fragile water supply. Curiously, there's no evidence of palaces, temples or monuments, leading archaeologists to speculate that it might have been ruled by elected officials or elites from each of its various districts.

As a boy in India, I remember being fascinated by stories attempting to unravel the mysteries of this full-featured civilization, revealed by the discovery of the city's ruins in 1911. A succession of digs, restricted by the United Nations since 1964 to help preserve the site, fueled plenty of classroom discussions about who these people might have been. Where did they come from? How did they build such an evidently well-planned and cohesive society, one that clearly had the strength to last for hundreds of years? And what happened to them? What sent them into decline and ultimately buried their cities for centuries? (Archaeologists and anthropologists think the Indus River changed course and, in doing so, changed the delicate balance with nature on which they survived.)

What we now call the Bronze Age was a fertile time for myths and mysteries in human history. During the centuries in which Mohenjo Daro flourished, the dynasties of the pharaohs were rising in Egypt, and pyramid building was in its heyday. The Chinese recorded the first year of their calendar, which now surpasses 4700 by most reckonings; the Jewish calendar was already more than a thousand years old by this point. The Code of Hammurabi was created in Babylonia. Stonehenge was a center of religious worship in England. By contrast, the Aztecs in Mexico and the Incas in the Andes Mountains of South America didn't show up on the world's stage for some seven hundred years and were still around when Spanish explorers colonized the New World for Europe in the 1500s.

Rituals were part of the discussions I remember from those years. Based on the evidence uncovered at the site, it was clear that Mohenjo Daro had some of the most intricately evolved rituals of any ancient society. Water and cleanliness were prominent among them, which is understandable since the civilization grew up along a river running through an arid region. What's more, like most agricultural societies, their rituals emphasized living in synergy with nature and celebrated the sun.

As do many of the world's great religions and cultures, Mohenjo Daro apparently had traditions and rituals that pointed its people toward the east. Why? Because that's where the sun came up, and its heat and light gave life to the whole day, just as its cycles organized the year. Look at any culture from past millennia, and you'll invariably find rituals based on the cycle of the sun's seasons. Celebrations of springtime, because that's the beginning of the time of growth, with its promise of the year ahead. Celebrations of fall, when the harvest comes in and people can rest and recuperate over the winter. In winter, as the days shortened and the sun's heat waned, ancient civilizations and religions built rituals around death and rebirth, in particular celebrating the anxiously awaited lengthening of the days, when the sun began again to track higher and stay longer, promising a new spring to come.

Though many of the rituals show similarities, each of these civilizations in its own way, and based on its own time and place, articulated different interpretations of why the world was what it was and operated the way it did. Over and over, those interpretations of reality differed so markedly that conflicts arose when two very different peoples eventually came into contact.

It Starts with Holiday and Family

Anthropologists as famous as Margaret Mead have long studied the effects of rituals on society. From the time we're children, through a celebration of specific rites, rituals link us to our immediate families, our communities, and our respective cultures. Obviously, religious traditions are a fertile source of rituals. But secular holidays also produce their share of rituals.

Consider New Year's Eve, arguably, the most ritual-ridden event celebrated by the world as a whole. In the U.S., all kinds of rituals are linked to the playing or singing of "Auld Lang Syne." The joke about this song is that it's the most popular tune that everyone sings but no one knows the lyrics to. But it is the most commonly sung song for English speakers on New Year's Eve. And, as rituals go, it's basically an accident.

"Auld Lang Syne" is an old Scottish song that was first published by the poet Robert Burns in 1796. But it was Canadian-born bandleader Guy Lombardo, not Burns, who popularized the song in the U.S. and turned it into a New Year's tradition. Lombardo first heard the song sung by Scottish immigrants in his hometown of London, Ontario. When he and his brothers formed the famous dance band Guy Lombardo and His Royal Canadians, the song became one of their standards.

In 1929, at a New Year's Eve party at the Roosevelt Hotel in New York City, Lombardo played the song at midnight, and a tradition was born. Eventually, his version was broadcast on radio and television, and in the decades that followed, right down to the present day, it has become a New Year's tradition for bands at parties to play the song at the stroke of midnight—and for attendees to do their level best to mangle the incomprehensible lyrics. As *Life* magazine once noted, if Lombardo failed to play "Auld Lang Syne," Americans wouldn't believe that the New Year had finally arrived.

While the English-speaking world is serenading itself with the worrisome prospect, "Should old (auld) acquaintance be forgot, and never brought to mind," however, the Japanese are working very hard to do just that. Forget, that is. Their New Year's holiday is called *Oshogatsu*, and it comes after a month-long effort to set the stage for a fresh start.

Throughout December, people hold *bonenkai*, or "forget-the-year" parties, as a way to prepare for the New Year. Misunderstandings and grudges are forgiven, and houses are cleaned in preparation for the future ahead. At midnight on December 31, Buddhist temples strike their gongs 108 times in an effort to expel 108 different types of human weakness.

Where much of the Christian world celebrates the Christmas holiday with cards of remembrance and elaborate gift-giving rituals, the Japanese conduct these rituals at the New Year. Children receive *otoshidamas,* small gifts with money inside, and their elders look forward to receiving New Year's cards from acquaintances. Provided they're postmarked by a certain date, the Japanese post office guarantees delivery of all New Year's cards by January 1.

Of course, what one civilization celebrates in midwinter another might have marked at another time of the year. The ancient Babylonians might have been the first to celebrate a New Year's ritual, but they did so on the first full moon after the vernal equinox: the beginning of spring in mid-March. (They're also believed to have been the first civilization to make New Year's resolutions.)

The Romans also celebrated a springtime New Year's until the transition to the Julian calendar around 46 BCE. But the ancient Egyptians focused their New Year's rituals on the middle of June, when the Nile overflowed its banks and brought rebirth to the land.

My point is that civilizations and religions and people in general can be tremendously diverse when we look at their underlying attitudes and beliefs. Yet their rituals—the behaviors that spring from those attitudes and beliefs—are fairly predictable and consistent. For example, you can see the same celebration of the circle of life in the wedding rings a Western couple places on each other's fingers and the procession around a fire in a Hindu wedding ceremony.

A few years ago, when my family and I toured the ruins of Pompeii, the legendary Roman city near Naples that was buried in volcanic ash in the first century CE, we were struck by how similar the urban landscape looked and felt for a traveler encountering it nearly two thousand years later. The way the houses were laid out, the way the streets connected, the orderly design of a long-forgotten city wasn't all that different from the way people live and work today. Life then mirrored life now: different attitudes and beliefs, but expressed through similar behaviors.

Behaviors That Become Rituals

Looked at from the reverse perspective, rituals gain power and importance in our lives precisely because they're a behavioral expression of our attitudes and beliefs. Different people from different cultural backgrounds, or points in time, or geographic perspectives, might share a common behavior—monogamous marriage, for example—but have different perspectives on what's going on and why. The involvement of parents and ancestors. The respective roles of husbands and wives. The place of children in the family. The sense of the permanence or impermanence of the vows being made. The willingness to entertain alternative arrangements. These might differ, but the essential behavior is two people committing to live and work together as one in a cohesive partnership.

There are plenty of good reasons for incorporating rituals into our lives, not least the sense of permanence and consistency they can represent within the overall context of an often chaotic world. Rituals are a way of coming to terms with the world. They assure us that we're not alone in feeling what we feel or doing what we do. Not surprisingly, we as marketeers have frequently found ways to articulate a form of comfort in familiarity through the way we position and promote our brands. It's similar to the comfort we as individuals find in the various cultures we belong to, from formal and informal communities to interest and ethnic groups.

In explaining the comfort of ritual, *The Handbook of Cultural Psychology* notes that emotion management is one of seventeen processes, divided into four broad categories, through which human beings "acquire culture": in a dictionary sense, the behaviors and beliefs characteristic of a specific group.[1] Neuroscientists tell us that more than 90 percent of what is going on in the human brain at any given time is below the level of conscious, rational thought. It's sensory, emotional, impressionistic. Managing ourselves within the structure of cultural norms calls for a broad set of coping skills in which ritual often plays an important part.

The four categories of processes laid out in the *Handbook* include:

1. **Reactive processes.** Various forms of conditioning, especially in infants and children, by which we learn to respond to and interact with the immediate world around us.

2. **Facilitative processes.** The more social forms of learning, including imitation, instruction, and collaboration.

3. **Psychodynamic processes.** Where we learn to link to what's like us, distance ourselves from what's not like us, and manage the often sudden and strong emotional experiences to which human beings are prone.

4. **Symbolic processes.** The uniquely human forms of "cognitive enculturation" in which we knowingly build a coherent view of our world and how it works.

The *Handbook* identifies symbolic processes, as well as instruction, collaboration, and emotion management, as being unique to humans. In the context of the last of those processes, the comfort of ritual is explained in a functional context:

> *Because unsettling inner experiences, including anxiety, fear, grief, rage, hunger, lust, and falling in love, are pervasive in life, human cultures provide rules and rituals that calm the anxieties associated with such experiences. This transforms a highly intense individual experience into a collective one, and it changes an experience that feels idiosyncratic and disturbing to one that is and has been shared by others.*[2]

Individualized Rituals

At first glance, all this talk about rituals might seem anachronistic. Don't we live in a world where the rituals of centuries past have been devalued, even lost? To some extent, yes—as a group phenomenon. When human life was more regimented, less centered around individual choices, rituals often were social phenomena that involved large groups of people. Just to keep them orderly and manageable, such rituals not uncommonly needed to assert a level of control that could become almost oppressively rigid: participants at a worship service standing or sitting or kneeling at the same time; people in meetings saying the same words or singing the same songs to affirm group values; wearing uniforms, some obvious (soldiers, public safety workers, medical personnel), some less so (like neckties for men in the workplace and skirts for women).

But even though many ritualized group norms have eroded over the years, we're still social creatures. We still respond to emotional cues. We crave connection, predictability, consistency, and control. One way we've typically found it is by giving at least some of the habits and routines in our lives a form of ritualized status. In the next chapter, we'll examine this progression from habit through routine to ritual from the standpoint of building brand-bonded behaviors. For now, consider how individuals can choose to give different status to the same basic actions.

For some people, drinking coffee is just a habit. For aficionados of Starbucks, Caribou, and the like, it can become a ritual. Getting dressed in the morning is a routine. Pulling out your lucky shirt or blouse or whatever for an important occasion can rise to the level of ritual. Giving someone a casual hug in the workplace or at a family gathering generally doesn't involve much thought. Tucking your children into bed at night can take on the trappings of ritual for both you and your progeny.

Just as they do in group settings, individuals find the use of ritual can be calming and relaxing, a way to focus intensity, a form of celebration, anything they want or need. Yoga and many forms of meditation, for example, tap a ritualized form of activity as a way to filter away distractions and bring someone into a certain place or state. Observers who don't share the individual's mindset or know their reason for investing so much importance in the behavior might be mystified, or even uncomfortable enough to resort to ridicule. Devotees understand.

Untapped Power Potential

In short, rituals are all around us. We might not always notice them or understand them if we do notice, but they're an intimate part of our lives. And they offer very real payoffs. Rituals are:

- **Comforting.** As noted above, we're wired to want to take the worry out of the "idiosyncratic"; making an important behavior consistently repeatable has that effect.

- **Reassuring.** Repeating an experience, and having it proceed according to your expectations, validates your choices and reinforces your confidence in your ability to make other decisions.

- **Time-efficient.** When you "know your lines," you can make the behavior work faster and more efficiently, which obviously has benefits in a time-starved world.

- **Special.** Not every habit or routine, or random action for that matter, has the potential to become a ritual; those that do are noteworthy because of the value they represent.

Rituals are a way, consciously or unconsciously, to restrict choices, which helps keep our lives manageable. As *The Handbook of Cultural Psychology* explains it, "behavior is regulated by culture in myriad ways that allow us to feel protected and accepted, and to fend off the anxiety that would come with having an infinite range of choices every moment of every day."[3]

Rituals, in other words, help make our lives both manageable and comfortable. They can make us feel good about the choices we've made, even though making the choices involved in our rituals precludes our making others, and thus possibly deprives us of new experiences that might be even more compelling or enjoyable. In a busy, time-starved world, too many choices can be as bad as too few. Many people today simply don't have time to sample and investigate and weigh a variety of options. Once they've made a decision, investing it with the importance of ritual frees up needed time for other choices while reinforcing their ability to make sense of a chaotic world.

Finding New Connections

The idea of rituals, specifically brand rituals, seems to be of interest to a few other people and organizations, albeit in a more episodic way. I have been among a select few espousing their potential, in my case since 1999. I have written articles, spoken about it at conferences, developed processes and methodologies, and created business models.

Others have looked into the idea in blogs over the past few years, as well. Stephen Denny, in the Marketing Profs Daily Fix Blog, talks about how rituals matter to us and how they play an increasingly important role for us as we steward our brands. In his mind, rituals define our groups and create a sense of community. We see people like us doing something that intrigues us and we copy their behaviors. On a personal front, rituals serve as centering touchstones, and in group settings, rituals create a means for effecting culture change. Denny transitions his discussions into how rituals can be used to build teams.

Mark Gallagher and Laura Savard, on their website Blackcoffee. com, had a post providing their definition of a ritual and how it can be a brand ritual. They talked about how a ritual can be a brand signal and a differentiator in a world of sameness.

The Marketing Practice blog, billed as the world's largest online resource on Indian brands, had a blog post by Harish B. Kochi in November 2007. He defined brand rituals as the performance of an act by the consumer as defined by brand owners. He believes that rituals are used as brand elements because of the stickiness effect and their ability to involve the customer with the brand. Rituals also create a pattern in the consumer's mind that triggers loyalty and acts as a differentiator. His guidelines for effective brand rituals are: simple, relevant, fun, consistent, and meaningful.

Krishna De wrote about how strong brands don't create rituals: their adorers do! In her Biz Growth News blog, she posited that the most powerful of the rituals or behaviors were not created or dreamt by marketers but by the adorers of the brand itself. She argues that a smart brand owner will uncover insights to determine what is at the root of the ritual and what it might mean for the further development of their brand.

In the Bidwell ID blog in November 2009, John Bidwell talked about turning routines into customs linked to your brand and about how humans like rituals because they are predictable and comforting. If they are unique, rituals offer an easy mental device for remembering something, and they help us form emotional connections. Bidwell defined some rules to consider, as well. Consistency. Relevance and simplicity. Giving customers control of the ritual.

All these episodic articulations are very consistent. All these strategists approach the concept of rituals and their development in very similar ways. They also use the same examples to make their point: Corona and its slice of lime; Guinness and its pour; New Zealand rugby team the All Blacks and their traditional dance, the haka.

From an agency standpoint, BBDO released a study in 2007 entitled (not entirely modestly) "BBDO—The Ritual Masters," in which it described the results of an agency project. As part of the study, BBDO's researchers asked more than five thousand people in twenty-one countries how they behave during five transitional periods of the day. While people in every culture reported engaging in rituals for similar reasons, as we've already noted, they approached them quite differently. About 41 percent of Chinese respondents said they schedule sex, for example, while only 3 percent of Russians and 7 percent of Americans do.

Key points of the study:

- **Rituals are universal.** In every part of the world, there are rituals that take people from sunrise to sleep and every phase in between each day. Each person repeats a series of actions to get himself or herself through the day. The only part of the puzzle that varies by geography is execution.

- **Fortress brands last and last.** Brands that have firm placement inside a ritual are known to have extensive "stickiness" with consumers and are therefore described as "fortress brands," brands so deeply associated with a particular ritual that they're tough to budge.

The five rituals BBDO identified as being performed most often by the most people worldwide are:

1. **Preparing for battle:** Like warriors getting ready for a fight, people approach the new day by emerging from their sheltering nighttime cocoons and getting themselves ready to face the outside world. According to BBDO's research, the most common task is brushing teeth (performed by 82 percent of people around the world), followed by:

- Taking a shower or bath: 74 percent

- Having something to eat or drink: 74 percent

- Talking to a family member or partner: 54 percent

- Checking e-mail: 54 percent

- Shaving (male): 53 percent

- Putting on makeup (female): 47 percent

- Watching TV or listening to the radio: 45 percent

- Reading a newspaper: 38 percent

Notably, 89 percent of people rely on the same brands when performing this sequence, and three out of four people say they become disappointed or irritated when their sequence is disrupted or their brand of choice is not available. For brands, this time of day represents the highest-volume opportunity, but it also is the ritual that is most entrenched and crowded.

2. **Feasting:** It's not surprising that eating with others ranks high among daily rituals. Americans are most likely to meet in a restaurant, whereas the Spanish and French are more likely to meet at home. For Saudis, Chinese, and Americans, the car has become a significant dining venue, with anywhere from 10 to 12 percent of people in these nations eating in their cars. (The global average is 7 percent.)

3. **Sexing up:** Under this indulgent ritual, individuals transform themselves from their everyday selves to their best selves. Then they set out to enjoy themselves in a variety of ways, eating and drinking luxury foods, forgetting diets, and generally treating themselves well. Typical respondents say preparation starts days before going out. Some call and talk about the evening ahead; teenage girls send photo messages to their friends with pictures of their outfits for approval and reassurance. Globally, more than three-quarters (78 percent) insist that sex itself is spontaneous. Yet 33 percent say that they reserve 10 p.m. to midnight for it, while more than 50 percent wait for the weekend. The Chinese are most likely to have "appointment sex" (41 percent vs. a global average of 9 percent).

4. **Returning to camp:** In contrast to the seven or more behaviors that are crammed into an hour of "preparing for

battle" at the start of the day, the "me time" moments when we're able to relax at day's end typically last an average of four hours and include fewer than five steps. This segment of the day typically begins around 8 p.m. and focuses on comfort. People get rid of or change all or part of their clothing: they kick off their shoes or get into their pajamas. Two out of three let go with media (66 percent watch TV in the evening); one out of five reads a newspaper; more than one-third go online. Many bathe or shower, a particularly popular activity among Brazilians (85 percent vs. the global average of 48 percent). Almost half of all people take something into the bathroom to read with them. Brazilians and Chinese read the most; Italians multitask. Few Americans (only 27 percent) are able to create time for themselves.

5. **Protection for the future:** The final prime area for rituals involves getting ready for the next day and taking a few extra steps to make sure family and property are safe. This is the time when people get their work clothes together for the next day, lay out luggage or briefcases for the ride to work or the airport, set the alarm, take their medication, or put a glass of water next to the bed. The series of rituals involved is considerably shorter, but it's no less critical. It enables the rituals of the next day. Reliable brands play a part in this.

Which Brands Fit?

I believe that in addition to one specific behavior that becomes ritualized, brands can become an integral part of their customers' regular behavior. Every time customers consider the category, this certain brand is the only one they will consider. To enable this state, brands need to deliver consistently engaging and enriching experiences that drive meaningful mindfulness and lead to consistent use of the brand.

For marketeers beginning to explore brand building and management in the context of ritual, it's important to start with an important caveat: not every brand qualifies for potential positioning as a ritual—and even for those that do, not every customer relationship can or should rise to the level of brand-bonded behavior. Seeing the differences between and the progression among habits, routines, and rituals will bring this distinction into sharp focus.

Endnotes

1. Shinobu Kitayama and Dov Cohen, eds., *The Handbook of Cultural Psychology* (New York: Guilford Press, 2007).

2. Ibid., 96.

3. Ibid., 97.

five

From Habits to Routines to Rituals:
THE CUSTOMER DECIDES

For some people, coffee is simply a habit. There's no thought to it. There's no personal involvement to it in the sense that they make a conscious choice to drink one kind of coffee vs. another, in one kind of setting vs. another, for one kind of an outcome vs. another. It's just something they do while they're thinking about doing something else.

For others, coffee is part of a fairly fixed and regular routine. When they get up in the morning, the first cup of coffee comes at a predictable point in time: after their shower, while they fix breakfast, before they make sure the kids get off to school on time. It's one of a chain of events in a familiar and time-tested sequence they enjoy and rely on whenever possible. At work, phone calls aren't returned, e-mails go unread, meetings have to wait until they have another hot cup of joe in front of them. In a restaurant, they expect their coffee to arrive before they're finished studying the menu and are ready to place an order; the meal isn't over until they've lingered over a final cup.

But deviations from their routines aren't unusual. They're permitted, even expected, and tolerated within the grand scheme of things.

But for some, coffee is a ritual: the day absolutely can't start without it. What's more, the "it" is a specific kind (or brand) of coffee, prepared or served or consumed in a specific way, with specific expectations for how it will make them feel as a result. With it, life moves forward smoothly and with confidence. Without it, the whole day gets off on the wrong foot and they might feel out of sorts for half the morning or longer. In familiar environs, they will organize their day to make sure they include their coffee at the desired time and in the desired way. On the road, they'll do whatever they need to do to figure out how to replicate their morning ritual in unfamiliar surroundings. They're personally involved, emotionally engaged, caught up in an act that has deep personal meaning and undeniable personal relevance. That ritual might make no sense at all to the casual observer, but its stature and importance are no less real to those committed to it.

Seeing the Progression

For marketeers, understanding this progression from simple habit to comfortable routine to cherished ritual is the key to seeing the true power and promise of this concept. The best way I've found to visualize it is with the graphic below, which I call an Experience Progression. It illustrates a stair-step form of progression in which, at each stepped-up level, participants' personal involvement with the branded product or service enriches their experience, in the process driving their level of brand commitment to ever higher levels.

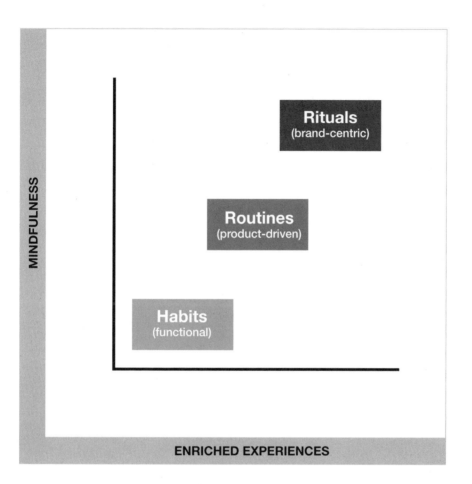

An obvious and familiar example is Starbucks. If coffee is simply a habit for you, Starbucks is likely to be just a coffee shop—and probably an overpriced one at that. If coffee's a routine for you, Starbucks is probably a familiar and trusted place to go to get it, but so, too, are Caribou, Dunkin' Donuts, Perkins, Denny's, and a host of other individual and chain purveyors of hot caffeine in a cup.

If, however, Starbucks is a form of ritual for you—as it is for me—you get more than just a regular venti coffee, double cup with a sleeve, and room for cream and four sugars when you turn away from the counter. You might notice a palpable sensation of satisfaction amid the familiar sights and sounds and smells and flavors you experience. You might subconsciously—perhaps even consciously—find yourself borrowing the famed L'Oreal tagline: sure, it may cost a little more . . . but I'm worth it. Because of the way it makes you feel, you might go miles out of your way to get your Starbucks rather than go to any of the alternative coffee places available to you. It's not just about coffee in a cup, so many ounces of an enjoyable beverage. It's about the experience of consuming that specific size and type and style of coffee in your own personal way.

Note how personal involvement changes as we work our way up the scale of interaction. Habits typically have very low levels of personal involvement. The brand is pushed out to the customer, but the customer doesn't give much back to the brand. Choices are fewer and more commoditized. The amount of thought required for the customer to successfully do what needs to be done is minimal. In many cases, participants aren't even aware of what they're doing. They're just going through the motions.

Routines step up to a medium or moderate level of involvement, typically focused on efficiency. In contrast to habits, this is a "customer-in" transaction. The customers make choices, but they generally involve very little involvement from or interaction with the business. Going through the drive-through and picking up a Number 7 is a routine: the customer has made a choice among alternatives, but it's a commoditized choice that the business can deliver with a minimum of customization. Speed is a virtue. Satisfaction is more a function of nothing in general going wrong than of something specific going right. The brands involved at this level are largely interchangeable: customers might have favorite places where they go for gasoline or groceries or a breakfast bagel, but they don't feel they *have* to go there. Lots of places will do.

Rituals are distinguished by extremely high levels of involvement, and that involvement is two-way: just as in other important relationships in people's lives, the principals must be able to interact capably and for their mutual benefit. That interaction, in turn, becomes part of the enriched brand experience, adding a layer of personalization to the brand's basic offering style. And as the experience is repeated, as the number of interactions grows, the bonds that define the relationship are strengthened. Now when something goes wrong, as it inevitably will, there's a resilience that allows the relationship to recover and continue. Instead of being alienated by the bump in an otherwise smooth pattern, the value the customer gives to the ritual provides a justification for their coming back. They're more willing to forgive—provided the brand enables that willingness and rewards it with renewed commitment to mutual satisfaction.

Seeing the Power

As we've already noted, not every type of customer activity has the potential to rise to the level of ritual, nor should it. Even in behavioral categories where the potential exists, not every interaction with a branded product or service can or should take on ritual significance for a given customer, if for no other reason than that the customer often doesn't want it to. But when a brand establishes itself as an intimate and valued element in a customer's life, it has a staying power that's both individually bankable and exploitable in recruiting other customers to the fold.

That's the power of ritual: it helps transform feelings into behaviors—behaviors that can endure even when the attitudes surrounding them change. And behaviors that can spread and inspire others to seek and enjoy similar benefits, building similar levels of loyalty to and advocacy for the brand.

But there's an important caveat that needs to be emphasized here, and it strikes at the very heart of marketing as we've known and practiced it in the past half century. The key to understanding the model of Experience Progression shown here is seeing it from the *customer's* point of view. Businesses don't unilaterally create brand rituals. Often, it's customers who do—whether or not they are enabled and supported by the business.

Similarly, businesses don't unilaterally control the conditions, the attitudes, or the contexts with which their brands are purchased and judged. (As we've seen, it's not for lack of trying.) What the customer brings to the encounter is also important, in some respects more important to long-term loyalty and repurchase patterns. And the conditions we've been exploring, from time starvation and sound–bite–based decisions to customers empowering themselves to accept or ignore what a brand offers based on their years of experience with it, all play active roles in that regard.

As a result, rather than seeking to extend and enhance their level of control over the circumstances in which their brands are marketed, marketeers intrigued by the prospect of encouraging brand rituals need to subtly shift their focus to creating conditions that enable their customers to invest the brands they favor with ritualized stature. That means seeing more than just the numbers: sales figures, transactional growth, marketing exposures, staffing costs, fulfillment obligations, repurchase rates, complaint resolutions. It means understanding why some brands are able to embed themselves in the customer's psyche while others are dismissed as colorless and interchangeable commodities.

Which means watching, listening to, understanding, indulging, and otherwise paying attention to how customers experience the brand on a behavioral level. In the context of the top-down hierarchies for which corporations are deservedly notorious, this might not come naturally, but it has the potential to pay off in a myriad of ways.

Placing a lime in the neck of a Corona bottle wasn't an idea created by marketeers at the Mexico City headquarters of Grupo Modelo, which brews the brand. But the company had the good sense to get behind it and support the idea in its marketing, and now it has become the "normal" way for consumers to get their Coronas.

Twisting apart the two halves of an Oreo cookie didn't originate with Nabisco brand managers any more than breaking a Kit Kat bar in two required someone at Hershey's to demonstrate how to do it. But as marketeers have shown themselves adept at encouraging something customers were already doing, they've embedded a behavioral image among the attitudes that keep their customers loyal.

In the case of Starbucks, it's the high level of personal involvement possible for the customer that drives the ritual aspects. How do they enable me to build a ritual? They create a full-featured setting that engages my senses in a variety of ways.

- The sight of many different kinds of coffee, each labeled and augmented with information (strength, characteristics, country of origin) to make it clear that I am being empowered to choose among a wide spectrum of desirable offerings.

- The sounds of espresso shots and coffee grinders and people talking about coffee.

- The aromas from coffees being ground and brewed and served.

- The interaction with someone who's knowledgeable about coffee, an enthusiastic barista preparing my coffee my way, not a bored "waitron" pouring an indifferent brew.

- The aura of community that tells me I'm standing among other people who also enjoy having a variety of attractive choices for the kind of coffee they desire.

- Tables, chairs, fireplaces, wall hangings, point-of-purchase impulse offerings—all of them chosen and arranged to help me create an experience that satisfies *me*, that rewards *me* for my higher level of involvement, that makes *me* look forward to coming back and repeating the experience. Soon.

- And don't forget the role of continuing innovation: adding new flavors, introducing new point-of-purchase sale items, and coming up with new supporting elements for the experience all are ways Starbucks works to create a higher level of mindfulness.

Starbucks then allows me to order my very own version of brew. This gives me my own personal, specific, customizable experience of coffee. This is the way I like it. It's unique and engaging for me. Because of the amount of personal control and meaning I can incorporate—even within the context of an enterprise that has to adhere to defined cleanliness standards, hire and train the staff, make payroll, pay the rent, and all the other requirements of day-to-day business operations—Starbucks has created the conditions that enable me to build a ritual.

Of course, as an empowered customer, I could create an equally satisfying ritual around making my own Starbucks coffee at home. Rituals don't require a store setting, or personal interactions, or a direct exchange of dollars for value to develop their power. If the coffee I buy, bag or can, preground or whole bean, enables me to create a consistently satisfying experience in the privacy of my own home, it, too, can rise to the level of a ritualized relationship. I have control. I invest what I do in brewing my own pot of coffee with personal values and expectations that are rewarded and reinforced when I pour myself a cup and sit down with the morning paper or my children to enjoy a carefully guarded half hour of quiet time before setting off to the daily workplace grind.

If I'm just brewing a pot of coffee and any old coffee at any old time will do, that's a habit. If the coffee I brew fits into other things I do almost on automatic pilot, it's a routine. But if I use the coffee I brew in specific ways to deepen my enjoyment of a given moment in my busy life, I'm creating a ritual.

Adding a Third Dimension

To add another element of context to the mix, our discussion of the differences among habits, routines and rituals also has to take into account frequency of use. Marketeers have to understand not only the level of personal involvement customers desire with their brands but also how often they're interested in repeating the ritualized experience.

All three types of brand experiences are repeatable. But they have different impacts on brand commitment:

- Repeating habits doesn't tend to move the needle on brand commitment. If anything, the lack of conscious choice and personalization reinforces the notion that it doesn't matter which choice the customer makes. They're all good enough to get by.

- Repeating routines tends to reinforce brand commitment, but on more of an unconscious level. Because a routine is based on a one-way, customer-driven quest for simplicity and convenience, repeating it serves to eliminate some alternatives while confirming the acceptability of others. "Good enough to get by" morphs into "a better option for what I need now."

- Repeating rituals, on the other hand, confirms the customer's decision that this is the best possible solution—for them.

Having weighed a number of choices, they've found the one that "gets them." And every time they reexperience that particular brand, their loyalty deepens as it reconfirms the reasons they chose it in the first place.

Here's a real-world example. Jos. A. Bank is a men's retailer. It doesn't sell anything I can't find at Nordstrom, Brooks Brothers or Macy's, or any number of other stores in the nearest regional shopping center or strip mall. But for me, shopping at Jos. A. Bank has become a ritual. Prior to discovering it, clothes shopping was a routine, and one I didn't much enjoy. Over time, suit coats start to show their age. Pants don't fit as well. Shoes wear out. A couple of times a year, I'd have to go looking for replacements, often with my wife along because I relied on her to help me make good choices.

One day, I walked into a Jos. A. Bank. It wasn't because of advertising or marketing. I hadn't seen a commercial, or received a coupon or sale notice in the mail or online. It was one of those classic accidents: I happened to find them because they were right next door to my bank. I walked in, and what I suddenly realized was freedom. I didn't need to dread shopping. I didn't need to work around my wife's schedule. I went into this store. I found a size that fit. I found salespeople who understood how I wanted to look in business settings. I found everything I needed: suits, shirts, ties, belts, shoes, the works. I was blown away.

And repeat experiences have only served to confirm and deepen the ritual nature of what I feel for this brand. It starts with the consistency I find when I repeat the experience. My suit size is 40 Short. Whether I go to the store in Naperville, Illinois, that I first wandered into, stop by a location while on the road, or order online, I've found that the 40 Shorts I buy from Jos. A. Bank fit me perfectly. Every time. The same is true for shirts, pants, shoes—you name it. I have complete confidence in both the quality of what they offer and the abilities of their people to help me make good choices. Consequently, I haven't bought a single piece of clothing from anywhere but Jos. A. Bank in the past five years.

Frequency reinforces ritual value, provided, of course, that there's consistency in the ritual as experienced. My loyalty to Jos. A. Bank isn't set in stone. If the quality of its products drop. If the same sizes fit me inconsistently. If the sales staff is dumbed down or incented in ways that don't serve my specific interests. In short, if something changes in a way that I don't personally accept and find value in, I'm gone.

Now That You Know, What Do You Do?

Brand rituals aren't for everybody. They're not a silver bullet, a magic weapon that solves every problem in every circumstance every time. But they are a way to strengthen the bedrock, committed customer relationships on which you can build a successful, enduring business.

To do so means accepting that a lot of things we've come to take for granted have changed. Control now has to be shared with customers. Information now has to be communicated piecemeal and in sound bites, not according to storylines we create and rigidly adhere to. Different customers now need to be reached in different ways. The power of mass marketing to one homogenous audience is in decline.

Most important, the fixation on customer acquisition, often at the expense of customer retention, needs to be refashioned into a new approach that emphasizes deepening and extending the base of knowledge we have about who our best customers really are and what they really want us to be doing on their behalf: the value equation they'll reward us for solving with the ultimate desirable behavior—buying from us again and again.

In the chapters that follow, we'll look at how marketeers can make that happen.

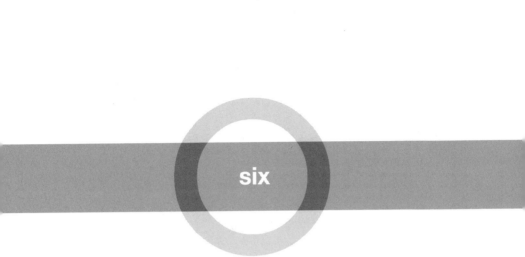

six

Working the Intersections

One of the situational blind spots in trying to diagram a dynamic continuum is a tendency to focus on specific points, often at the expense of the bigger picture. We like to look for the signs that say "you are here," and we like that "here" to have some specific orientation so we can see where we've come from and where we're going.

In the model introduced previously, I've tried to provide a visual representation of where loyal customers fall in their use of brands, from those whose involvement is somewhat casual and essentially unconscious to those who have made a conscious decision to weave our brands into their routines—but without any emotional commitment or loyalty—to those at the high end of the scale, where there is only one brand that will satisfy their ritualized desire by building a bond.

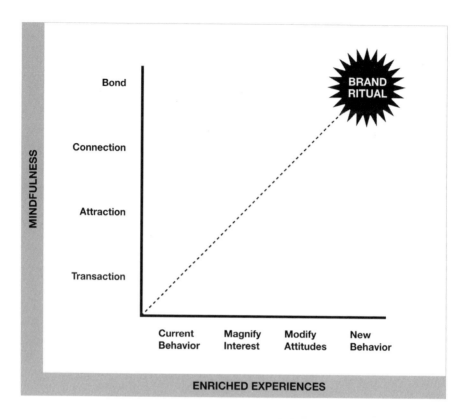

In this chapter, we're going to look at the intersection points where the customer experience changes: from initial use to a habit, from an unconscious habit to a conscious routine, and from a conscious routine to a bonded ritual—ultimately to become an established and difficult-to-dislodge pattern of intensely loyal, ritualized behavior. As we explore these intersection points, it will be important to understand three key principles:

1. **Every business has customers at each stage along the continuum.** To a significant extent, customers decide which point along the continuum is most comfortable for them in their experience of the brand. Not every customer,

in other words, wants to have a bonded relationship with every brand; that level of emotional intensity simply isn't sustainable in our time-starved, sound-bite-driven world. That said, however, loyalty becomes more intense and more stable as customers proceed up the continuum toward that level of ritual. Consequently, there is a valid reason for creating systems and managing expectations in ways that will enable them to move toward a form of ritualized bonding with the brand.

2. **While businesses have customers at all points along the spectrum, specific customers inhabit just one point.** They might be casually loyal to the brand. Or they might be emotionally and experientially bonded with it. But their loyalty can be plotted along this continuum. And we can use a variety of evidence to learn more about what cues they're responding to as their relationship with the brand grows through continuing experiences. Some of that evidence is formal and shows scientific rigor, like brand bonding research; some is informal and largely anecdotal, like the online tracking insights that savvy businesses are learning to mine in greater detail.

3. **The comfortable assumption that we can and should nurture customers along an orderly progression no longer reflects the real world.** As we've seen, for businesses struggling to market brands and manage customer experiences in a time-starved, sound-bite-driven world, it pays to be quick on your feet and prepared to take advantage of opportunities as they present themselves. More than ever before, marketeers must react instantly to changing conditions, which means both prepositioning sound bites to be accessible when the customer wants information and using

today's almost instantaneous digital tools to anticipate customer wants and needs, or at least respond to them as rapidly and effectively as possible.

Two Ways to Respond

The axes along which we can plot changing customer loyalty are important in this regard. The vertical axis we've labeled "Mindfulness," which is a term that's worth defining in this context. The horizontal, which we've called "Enriched Experiences," challenges marketeers to think like operational managers, a thought pattern that might help us regain some of that lost access to those who make day-to-day and long-term decisions in our organizations.

Certainly, in our busy world, "keeping our heads in the game" is a constant concern. That's doubly true for customers. With time at a premium and information highly fragmented, we necessarily have to do so many things today virtually on automatic pilot that when someone wants us to pay attention, our first response might be to resist. After all, we only have so many brain cells to go around, and a lot of them are already committed to the various things we're multitasking our way through in the course of the day.

How often do you find yourself walking in the door at work and wondering how you got there? Were the kids dressed for school before you left? Was the dog fed? Did you water your plants? Turn off the coffee pot? Lock the door? If your computer fails to boot up this morning or your cellphone goes dead, will you have any clue what's on your schedule for the day? Who was it you were supposed to call before 10 o'clock? Do you have a meeting over lunch? Were you going to bring your lunch? Is there even going to be time for lunch?

For brands, mindfulness increasingly is one of the most powerful differentiators along the continuum from casual exposure to ritual.

If customers aren't really making a conscious choice about where to stop for coffee, or where to shop for clothes, or which brand of whatever to order, their loyalty is both fragile and undependable. While they can build a lifestyle that way, we can't build a bankable business on such constant change. Every time customers look at a specific situation, consider a specific need, or react to a specific stimulus, we want our brand to be the only specific choice they consider.

Increasing customer mindfulness is one way to accomplish that. If you think about it for a moment, you'll find you interact with a large number of brands in the course of your day. Some you're mindful of. Some you aren't. How can you tell the difference? The former you'd miss if somehow they weren't available when you wanted them. The latter you probably wouldn't: some other brand would surely be available to fill the basic bill. Mindfulness is one of the things that differentiates a habit from a routine and a routine from a ritual.

When I want coffee, I want Starbucks. I make a conscious choice to look for a store where I can find what I know I want and will enjoy. Despite the time pressures of the day, I'll even go out of my way to find a Starbucks, in the process passing everything from competing coffee merchants to restaurants and kiosks to convenience stores that offer some form of brew.

What's true for an everyday choice is as true for something a little more special. When I want new golf clubs, I want Pings. (I am a fanatical golfer.) When I considered buying a new car recently, the only brand I had eyes for was BMW. And it's as true for intangibles as tangibles. When I'm online looking for information, I consciously choose to run my searches through Google. These brands are now indispensable parts of my life because I've made a conscious, mindful choice to use them to the exclusion of any other alternative.

On the other hand, it's worth noting that we can and do develop ritualized experiences around even the most prosaic of choices. It's not just a matter of selectively looking for specific high-end products or cutting-edge services. I confess I have a thing for Eggo waffles. If I have time for breakfast at home, that's what I want to find in my freezer. On more than one occasion, I've actually skipped breakfast when we were out of strawberry Eggos. That's the hold a brand can have on a customer when it engages mindfulness in a meaningful way.

What engages and enhances mindfulness, in turn, is experience—the more involving and enriched, the better. This is the behavioral attribute that trumps all the attitudinal positioning in the world. It's the essential ingredient in virtually all of the lasting relationships in our lives, from the organizations we work for to the friends we value to the significant others we create families and homes with. The bonds that hold those relationships and others together, that make them stable over time and resilient when challenged, are the experiences that have tested and refined and strengthened the values and promises with which they have been built.

Those experiences not only make the relationship more solid and resilient, in some ways they also inoculate it against change. I've certainly been exposed to countless marketing messages for other coffees, other golf clubs, other cars, other search engines, other waffles. The claims generally strike me as credible, the alternative brands competent, the marketing messages clever, even professionally admirable. But the lens through which I necessarily view these competing claims is the one formed by my own experiences. The brands to which I've consciously chosen to be loyal have facilitated the creation of lasting bonds by the way they have allowed me to have enriched, personal experiences with them.

Taking the Easy Way to Profitability

And to the extent that they continue to allow that kind of relationship to deepen and grow, I'm going to do the simple, easy thing in a time-starved, sound-bite-driven world: I'm going to keep making the decisions I've already done the work for. After all, it's simpler, easier, more time-effective *for me* to repeat an established and comfortable behavior pattern than to budget the time and mind space to think through a new one.

Although it seems so simple and obvious when looked at from that perspective, many businesses are still so caught up in the chase for new customers that they miss the various efficiencies and advantages that can accrue to those that encourage long-term loyalty from the customers they've already fought for and won. The smart ones, on the other hand, continue to find ways to further enrich my experiences with them. They continue to tweak existing offerings and innovate to create new ones, in both ways increasing customer mindfulness in choosing the alternatives they represent.

When Starbucks adds new blends or offers new selections of music and snacks at their counters, it elevates my next experiences to a refreshed ritual. Google's different logos for different occasions register similarly on the mindfulness scale. Even Eggo knows simple doesn't excuse stagnant: it offers new and improved versions of its products to continue rewarding my loyalty.

This is where digital technology is rapidly becoming indispensable. Twenty years ago, futurists used to burble about a world where "n = 1." Today, we're there. When Amazon customizes recommendations based on my purchase and browsing history—modified by its understanding of customers with usage patterns similar to mine—it is looking for ways to enrich my continuing experiences. When Ping provides detailed information about the results of its research and how its clubs perform for golfers at my skill level, it is offering me a place in a dynamic community of like-minded and like-skilled individuals, not just encouraging me to add new clubs to my bag.

Ping certainly isn't alone. Tesco, the fourth largest retailer in the world, designed and continues to evolve its innovative Clubcard program not just as a way to track its customers' loyalty to the company but, more important, to also recognize its loyalty to its customers. Harrah's does it with sophisticated modeling that creates relevant, customized offers based on its customers' previous Harrah's gaming history. United Airlines uses partnerships and enhanced sets of services to improve the experience for United MileagePlus program members.

What these leading organizations do, any organization can learn to do. And every organization needs to. As we've noted before, cognition works—customers learn from experience. What I experience with Starbucks and BMW, Ping and Jos. A. Bank, Google and Eggo changes my expectations for every other brand competing for my business.

When it comes right down to it, experiences are the irreplaceable foundation stones of relationships. Promises don't build lasting bonds. Only performance does: real interactions that represent two-way exchanges for mutual benefit. And while interpersonal relationships grow stronger and more resilient from constant care and communication, brand relationships also need to find ways to reward and delight and continue to nurture customer loyalty. The occasional flowers and jewelry and surprise weekend away from it all are the special personal touches that add yet another level to the texture of enriched experiences that give a relationship its staying power.

Deconstructing the Intersections

As brand experiences move up the continuum toward rituals, we can plot four specific stages. Each reflects a form of steady progression. On the Mindfulness (vertical) axis, customers proceed from basic transactions, which might involve very little considered thought or emotional involvement, to ones for which there is real attraction, to a point where a definite connection is made, and finally to a level where they are bonded to the brand.

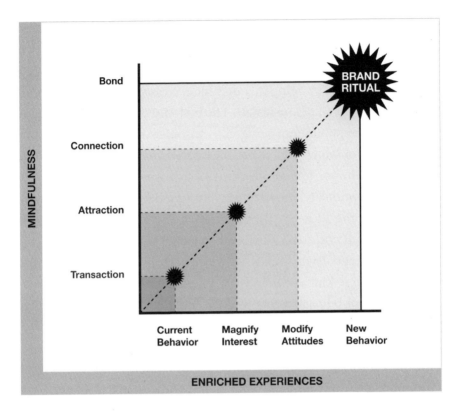

On the horizontal axis, enriching experiences move them from a basic level of current behavior to a magnified level of interest, where they begin to invest themselves more in what the brand is promising, to a level where their attitudes toward the brand itself begin to change—a point of both power and peril, as we'll see in a moment. Ultimately their behavior itself becomes deliberate and personally invested in what the brand is promising them.

Here's what at stake at each stage.

Stage one: intersection of current behavior and transactions: Customers have to start their experience with us somewhere. Their first stage of involvement with a brand is that initial transaction, which represents a change in their current behavior in the sense that they have chosen to use something new and different. They might have done so based on your conventional marketing efforts. However, as we've seen, they might have come to you as a result of a sound bite that induced them to give you a try: an unsolicited recommendation from a friend or colleague, a posting in a user blog, a casual discovery based on their keywords for an online search. The best-laid plans are important, to be sure. But serendipity can bring you customers in ways you've never anticipated or for which you've never prepared yourself (let alone them).

We've known for decades that word-of-mouth recommendations are exceptionally powerful, of course. But in our increasingly digital world, the idea of "friend" itself is in flux. We have friends we've interacted with over time on a personal, face-to-face level. But nowadays we also have friends we've never physically met. Despite the fact that these kinds of friends are essentially total strangers, people nonetheless will rely on their opinions and value their recommendations similarly to bona fide friends'.

Increasingly, marketeers are seeing intriguing evidence that customers who sample others' opinions form judgments and take actions with a high level of confidence, despite not knowing the true sources of the information available to them. Businesses continue to learn, often to their chagrin, that a simple comment left unaddressed in a forum or posted unchallenged to a third-party blog can almost overnight take on a life of its own—often with profound consequences for the business. (Remember the busted-up guitar that inspired one unhappy United passenger's three-song lament.)

On the positive side, almost everybody enjoys sharing a favorite brand experience with friends and colleagues: a great place to eat, an undiscovered entertainer, a surprisingly well-designed and managed customer experience. This new definition of friendship enhances that dynamic.

For me, my Ping G15 clubs are a working example: in recent years, I've made a number of "converts" to the joys of playing golf with Pings. Ping doesn't pay me to do that. I don't receive a "spiff" for convincing people about their features and benefits or encouraging them to try their clubs. But I derive some very real personal satisfaction when someone I've encouraged to try them turns out to share my passion because it helps their game, and that just adds to the power of the ritualized bond I feel toward the brand.

First impressions are powerful and lasting, especially in our constantly connected world. When your brand has an opportunity to convert someone else's customer, however loyal, to your extended family, it has to be ready to respond by delivering on the core promises you've been making for it.

In order to get the consumer into that necessary initial transaction, we need to use what I call the New Value Equation (NVE). The New Value Equation takes into account the changes that have swept the economic landscape and the reorientation of consumer priorities that has followed.

$$\text{NVE} = \frac{\text{PF} + \text{DVD}}{\text{CP}}$$

The New Value Equation (NVE) is product features (PF) plus differentiated value drivers (product quality, customer service, and added-value offers) divided by competitive price (CP). This equation is a robust way for consumers to make a decision that is right for them. It acknowledges their individuality and their need for specific product and service requirements. It also gets you the first transaction in a way that improves the odds of their moving up to the next stage of the process.

Stage two: intersection of magnified interest and attraction: This is where consistency becomes an important attribute in the new customer's growing experience with your brand. If that first trial, however tentative, earns you a repeat opportunity, you need to be able to build on and extend the positives of your brand promise to convince customers that their interest is justified, the decision they've made is sound, and their continuing loyalty will be rewarded.

In a way, the goal here is to consolidate and begin to widen the beachhead you've made, not to leap full-blown from a casual encounter to the equivalent of a twenty-year bond. You don't want to overwhelm new customers with dizzying levels of change and too many confusing choices. But you do want to show them your brand is more than a proverbial one-trick pony. As they learn more—not just through their own experience but through sound bites from others in your customer base—you are in essence giving them additional reasons to continue to buy your brand: different facets to explore, different configurations to enjoy, different prospects to anticipate for the future.

The most important action that brands need to take to magnify attraction is to become digital at their core. The key to working with customers at this intersection is to offer a wider spectrum of possibilities without inundating them. It's important to enlist the customer's own energy and interest in building the new bond, part of the basic two-way dynamic of successful relationships. Digital experiences for customers at this stage should deliver on the brand's core value proposition to provide new and different reasons for them to continue interacting with your brand, rather than slipping back into older habits they're just now leaving behind.

Stage three: intersection of connection and modified attitudes: Converting the initial transactional encounters that customers have with your brand into lasting relationships requires creating a true connection. They now have more than marketing messages and others' recommendations to aid their decisions. Their own experiences increasingly inform the choices they are making, in the process modifying their attitude toward your brand.

This is where mindfulness shows its power. The customers are beginning to build a sustainable connection with your brand. They want it. They like it. You're becoming a part of their lives. Whenever they turn to your particular category, your brand comes to mind first.

I want coffee? Starbucks. I want new golf clubs? Ping. I need a new suit? Jos. A. Bank. I need information? Google. I need merchandise? Amazon. The daily routines involved in being a customer are growing more consciously informed. Real choices are being made. Real loyalty is being established. This is the start of the long-term payoff for all your hard work in marketing.

But while this is a point of great potential, it's also a moment of real peril. In fact, more brands screw up here than at any other stage on the continuum. Having wooed and won, too many start to lose focus and move on to new conquests. New customers, having been attracted by visible levels of interest and activity from the brand, can now start to feel jilted, even betrayed, when they sense the luster dimming.

Many of us have had far from satisfying experiences with providers of information-age staples like cable television and cellphone service. The various providers involved commit countless dollars to entice their competitors' customers to switch. But once the providers have our signature on a new two-year contract, it's like they do everything but holler, "Gotcha, sucker!" and turn away in the pursuit of the next prospect.

Meanwhile, heaven help us if a new service configuration is introduced that offers a measurably better deal—more service for less money. When we were in the market, no promise was too heady for them to make. Now that we're locked in, forget it, buddy. You're stuck for the next couple of years. They could care less about taking care of you, let alone changing the terms of your agreement to reflect the better offer they're now making to competitors' customers. Guess you should have waited a little longer and resisted a little harder, huh?

For more than twenty years now, research on customer relationship management has documented again and again that it costs far more money to attract a new customer than it does to keep a customer you already have. But the thrill is in the hunt, so businesses continue to essentially walk away from all the initial goodwill they've earned with their customers rather than building on it to create something not only more lasting and more dependable, but more likely to stimulate still more enthusiastic word-of-mouth communication.

The goal, for any brand, is to become indispensable. That takes work. Lose your focus now and you can end up with dour, disgruntled customers who just can't wait to low-rate you to their friends, personal and virtual. Continue to treat them like they're important, on the other hand, continue to pay off on the brand promises you've been making, and they'll notice. And they'll appreciate it. And they'll tell people about it.

Savvy marketeers don't let up when they sense the customer has moved to this stage. They use the knowledge of their core customers to deliver meaningful innovations to deepen and broaden the customer relationship. Tesco's Clubcard draws on its growing database of purchase information to create different clubs, programs, and services that not only reward their customers for their loyalty, but also provide them with other reasons for their continuing business. Harrah's fine-tunes reward offers down to watching what time gamers take dinner breaks and what they prefer to eat. Best Buy's Reward Zone program is growing increasingly robust yet also increasingly personalized. United Airlines continues to look for ways to make its existing fliers fly more and have a better experience every time they fly. Meaningful and differentiated experiences deliver deeper connections with customers.

For established products, constant modifications can support this sense of a robust and well-designed brand offering. Note how even hot new products, like Apple's iPad, keep evolving with new versions while adding to the base of apps, how Starbucks routinely augments the blends it offers, how category leaders like Clorox add to the value of an outwardly simple product with new information designed to help customers make better and more productive use of the brand.

Stage four: intersection of brand bonding and new behavior: At this point, true brand-bonded behavior has been earned. This is when your brand is now part of the customers' ritual. The customer has only one conceivable choice: yours. What's more, not only can you count on continuing behavioral loyalty, you probably also have created an advocate for your brand. I've never been one to go out of my way to recommend specific products and services. But sometimes it amazes me to hear myself touting the performance of Ping irons or sharing wider insights and opinions on my travel experiences on United because of the immediate bond that seems to grow among its adherents.

Brand ritual behavior is about as bankable as anything you can get in our fast-changing world. These customers will insist on your brand, invest even some of their own limited time to make sure they find you when they want you. Not only does that pay off in making the cash register ring on a regular level, but it also provides a level of insulation against the blandishments of your competitors.

As we've noted, the very term "ritual" calls up an image of religious fervor, and brand-bonded behaviors can display a level of zealotry that corresponds in many ways. Customers with such deep and powerful feelings toward your brand are as unlikely to change their preferences on the spur of the moment as committed believers are to leave one church for a different denomination or religion.

At the same time, they are not mindlessly locked in. Having invested themselves in the relationship, they have expectations—about shared values, about levels of quality and commitment, even about things like corporate citizenship. In the summer of 2010, Target made a large contribution to a political advocacy campaign in its home state of Minnesota that advocated business values it supported. The gubernatorial candidate the campaign endorsed promoted those business values. He also had taken a position against same-sex marriage, however, and

Target has long prided itself on its open courtship of all aspects of the community in which they belong.

While other organizations had made similar contributions, the GLBT community's outrage focused on Target. And the company responded by affirming its business beliefs but also working to restore its good relationships with a community that had found it insensitive to other principles it professed to hold as deeply.

Similarly, after the catastrophic oil spill in the Gulf of Mexico, BP stubbed its corporate toes several times during the clean-up efforts. One byproduct: BP gas stations, many of them owned by individual entrepreneurs, not the corporation, saw their business decline as customers scapegoated their stations for oil-soaked beaches and hapless fish and wildlife thousands of miles away. As part of its corporate outreach, BP found it needed to spend significant amounts of money on marketing messages designed to clarify the working relationship between its station owners and the public.

The values the brand holds become the emotional glue that enables customers to believe in it and permit access into their daily lives. This is the deepest level of loyalty and the most sustainable. This is the level where your brand is part of their ritual. A brand ritual.

Brand rituals are not silver bullets. They're an outgrowth of a form of brand-bonded relationship that places definite obligations on organizations that seek to nurture and benefit from such intense feelings and behaviors. Building them requires careful planning and deliberate execution of well-designed marketing strategies, backed by operational tactics that remain consistent with the values the organization promotes to its customers.

The payoff for such relationships, however, is a level of customer loyalty that is likely to prove indispensable in global marketplaces where time is at a premium—and information is not.

seven

Delivering a New Value Equation

We have reached the juncture in our journey where we will move from discussing the need for change and even the process of change to the all-important concrete steps for change.

Up to this point, we've defined four distinct stages in developing a brand ritual. Reaching the ritualized state itself is the fourth of those, and sometimes a brand can reach it very quickly. But, more often, such intense loyalty must be built over time, one transaction at a time, as customers work their way up along the continuum we've explored previously.

- Before customers get to the highest level of loyalty, where brand rituals are realities, they have to develop a connection strong enough to modify their attitudes.

- Before those all-important attitudes change, their personal interest needs to be magnified to the point that they become positively attracted to your brand.

- And before that interest itself can be built into a powerful force, they first need to change existing behavior to give you that first transaction: their first opportunity to encounter your brand and judge whether it satisfies their needs and expectations.

Why four chapters to examine these stages? This is to counteract a very common misstep of ambitious marketeers. Often, they will attempt to fire on all four stages at once. They will try to use the same approach to each of these four stages. I don't recommend it. It pays to follow the process one might embrace when improving his or her golf game. As I mentioned in chapter 6, this is one sport I am fanatical about. You can't improve all aspects of your game in the same way all at once. Even the most aggressive pro would not suggest such an effort. Rather, the smart way to get better is to break down the overall game into attainable stages of success: First, get a consistent swing. Next, work on your short game. Then turn your focus to putting. And finally, learn course management. By taking the process in four steps and understanding that each of these requires a different approach, you improve your overall chances of success and begin steadily lowering your scores. Even if you haven't mastered all four, each aspect that you work on brings your overall game into sharper focus, improving the end result.

The trick is to work on each in its own way. The game's still going to frustrate you, of course. But taking an orderly approach to it will turn out to be much more productive in the long run than trying to do a little bit of everything without ever learning how to do any of them that well. As each part of your game gets stronger, you can move on to the next challenge. And, also like golf, developing brand rituals is a never-ending process.

If you look at your brand franchise, you will see a dispersion of your customers at each stage of the progression. As the chief marketeer, you need to figure out and prioritize the stage you want to address first. As with golf, each step is designed to give you the ability to move to the next one. You don't have to do everything; you need to do one thing well to move up to the next stage.

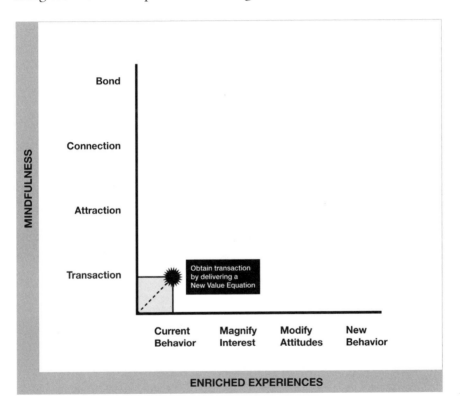

In this chapter, we'll focus on that first step. For marketeers, this is hardly new ground. Indeed, as we've seen, the art and science of marketing have been focused for decades largely on the quest to attract new customers. Nothing in this analysis is meant to say we don't still have to do that: a brand that doesn't attract new customers is a brand that's withering and ultimately dying.

But this important step is just the beginning. This chapter will provide the construct on how we can deliver this first stage in the process. It will lay out the need to embrace the New Value Equation and also provide examples of companies already achieving success with this approach.

Getting Started

To get our prospect into our franchise, whether it is a retail store, an e-commerce site, or a service opportunity, we need to find that first hook. We need to get the prospect to change his or her current behavior (use of another category or competitive brand) so we can win that first transaction.

How do we do that? Certainly not the way we might have in previous business cycles. In days gone by, it would have been reasonable for us to follow the path laid out by the traditional value equation.

$$\frac{\textbf{Product Features}}{\textbf{Lowest Price}} = \textbf{Old Value Equation}$$

This has been the popular value equation for many decades. It was the construct that propelled innovation as creators of goods and services competed to introduce new and improved products across all categories and do a better job than the next guy of delivering great product features to the consumer. As a result, food got better, toiletries got better, technology got better, cars got better, medicines got better, and our quality of life improved.

But it was also an equation ruled by price. Innovations were often quickly copied and so their benefits were short lived. If you had dry-roasted Folgers Coffee selling at $3.99 a pound, you might see Maxwell House come along with fire-roasted Maxwell House Coffee at $3.99 to make a grab for market share. It was all about the product features that were available at the lowest price. Since any new product features were often quickly copied, lower price drove consumer behavior almost every time.

This has been the paradigm for quite some time. But in the past two decades, the ground has shifted. We have been roiled by two recessions, the first after 9/11 and the second that ran from 2008 to 2010. These events rewrote the rules for businesses and marketeers. The 2008 recession has been described as the worst economic crisis since the Great Depression, and its impact on consumers has been significant and long lasting. A number of companies have done a lot of research to understand consumer attitudes and behaviors during this period. This information applied to my personal experiences with consumers during this period, provide compelling insight into the changes wrought. The events of the two economic contractions propelled the consumer into a crisis. Not a crisis of money, as would be expected, but into a crisis of anxiety. Understanding the nature of the crisis is important to understanding the changes in consumer behavior.

What we see is that the consumer today does not feel broke so much as afraid. The world as the consumer knew it has been upended. Things that seemed inalienably true—a home is a fail-safe investment, the stock market will keep rising, my job is secure, I will have enough money for retirement—are all called into question. We see consumer anxiety at very high levels. It doesn't matter whether you're young or old, rich or middle-class, man or woman. There is no buffer from this trauma.

As a result of this fear, consumers have begun to change their behaviors. They are staying home more. They are putting off major purchases. They are managing their personal expenses better by lowering the heat and opening up windows. Their gifting behaviors have changed. It is about more personal connections versus materialistic excesses.

Additionally, they are more comfortable looking for bargains. Women will spend hours trolling through numerous stores to get the right dress—at 50 percent off. A guy will visit eBay every day for weeks until he can find an iPad at a bargain price. A family decides to buy the used car instead of the new one. Within all these demographic groups, we begin to see a new theme. They are all willing to make the effort required to find what they need at the right value.

What's more, the very definition of value is undergoing a transformation. Unlike the past, where the traits of value were product features for the lowest price, the traits consumers associate with value are different today. They are more interested in the quality of the product. They want stuff that's going to last. They also want to be assured that the company will service the product in case there are issues with it. Additionally, they would like to get some extra value-added benefits from the product. With all these other expectations, lowest price, which over the past few decades was the most important discriminator, is now less so. Price is no longer the most important factor in defining value.

It is not surprising that consumers view price in this way. Opinions of price competitiveness and parity have been greatly shaped by the advent of technology. Today I can check the price of anything easily. In a few clicks, I can uncover the entire pricing model of any product. Because this information is so readily available, price has become a commodity. No company can price its wares without being fully aware its price can be checked, compared, and contrasted with every other brand in the category in a matter of minutes. When price becomes a commodity, it is no longer the only signal of a good deal.

So what has taken its place?

The New Value Equation

The old value equation needs to be replaced by the New Value Equation (NVE) I mentioned in the last chapter. The New Value Equation takes into account the changes that have swept the economic landscape and the reorientation of consumer priorities that has followed. It looks like this:

$$\frac{\text{Product Features} + \text{Differentiated Value Drivers}}{\text{Competitive Price}} = \text{New Value Equation}$$

Product features (PF) plus Differentiated Value Drivers (DVD—product quality, customer service, and added-value offers) divided by competitive price (CP). This New Value Equation is a robust way for consumers to make a decision that is right for them. It acknowledges their individuality and their need for specific product and service requirements.

Let's look at each of these in more detail.

Competitive Price

It's important to note the change in the common denominator. No longer is "lowest" price the critical differentiator. Now the customer wants to know he or she is getting a "competitive" price. It might not be the lowest, but it needs to feel appropriate, reasonable, and palatable to the customer, who will weigh it along with the other attributes when making a buying decision.

A good example of the "competitive" price offer in action can be found in the programs Progressive Insurance created a number of years ago. Progressive provides insurance products and competes against some of the giants in the category. It is not the biggest, the first mover, or the most obvious choice for car insurance. In order to get consumers to stage one—to pull the trigger on that initial transaction—Progressive understood the consumer concern around value and provided a solution that went to the very heart of this new view on pricing. In addition to revealing its own pricing structure, Progressive provided the consumer the prices from its competition. Sometimes, the Progressive price was the lowest. Sometimes it was not. But the act of revelation was powerful. It said to the consumer: "You can trust me." Already, Progressive was known in the industry as a quality provider of auto insurance. By promoting its willingness to provide this level of price transparency, the company was able to set itself apart from the competition. With this move, Progressive made a direct appeal to consumers who were no longer married to buying on "lowest price" but were deeply committed to buying on "competitive price" as long as their other needs were met—in this case, the ability to trust the insurance provider. Progressive not only showed that its prices were competitive. The program went further in displaying a deep and cutting-edge understanding of the customer mindset.

The New Definition of Quality

With price moved to a lesser rung on the ladder, quality has moved up and become more important. In the New Value Equation, quality plays a starring role. Yet it is not the standard definition of quality that marketeers might have been used to. It is one that has evolved and forced providers of goods and services into new and more sophisticated constructs.

Simply put, the consumer today wants what feel like premium-quality products and services for a competitive price. This seems like a demanding mindset, but with a wave of companies stepping up to deliver just that combination, it's clear to all that quality at a mass price is not only possible, it is the new normal.

Target was one of the first to create this new paradigm in its business many years ago. Within the framework of a discount chain, it began to inch up the quality of its merchandise and, more important, the quality expectations of its customers. Target framed this offering with its "expect more, pay less" proposition. And consumers responded. Shoppers at Target did not feel as though they were digging for change in the couch cushions. They viewed the retailer with respect and appreciation. They called it Targét, a faux French pronunciation for a store with Midwestern roots. All this conveyed the new perception of quality—good stuff at a good price. It was a deal the consumer demanded, and Target delivered.

Target set the bar for brands a number of years ago. It took a long time, but now this expectation has become part of the consumer mainstream. In the New Value Equation, all brands that want to succeed in today's economy have been compelled to do the same. Many are doing so across a number of different industries with success. Ford provides features that were once reserved for luxury cars in its economy vehicles—everything from GPS to voice-controlled functions to factory-installed iPod adapters. Crest delivers high-end teeth-whitening technology in a toothpaste. Jos. A. Bank sells 100 percent wool suits for under $500. Bridgestone provides ball fitting to improve your golf game. These reflect the new mindset of the consumer when it comes to quality. Consumers expect brands to provide quality so they know the products will last. We are evolving from a society that was willing to dispose of stuff quickly to one that plans to keep purchased items for a long time. With this shift in mindset, quality has become not just a standard for luxury brands; it has become table stakes for all brands that want to be considered. Every brand needs a compelling and credible quality message, or it will have to sit out the game.

The quality imperative has spread throughout industries. Old-line brands have stepped up: Campbell's unveiled an ad campaign touting its natural ingredients. New brands also have embraced the mindset to take off: JetBlue pressed its case with the tag line "No first class seats. No second class citizens." The message there was crystal clear: quality was the right of all JetBlue passengers. Why would anyone agree to pay for less than the best?

Great Customer Service

Not only do consumers insist on quality, they also insist that companies stand behind their quality promises. This is where we see the increased importance of customer service in the consumer decision-making process. Customer service, in the context of the New Value Equation, is much more than a smile and a "Have a nice day." It is a current that runs through the entire transaction and one that the customer expects to be fresh and available at all times—24/7, even years after the purchase is made. Customer service is not window dressing on the transaction; it is an important factor in how customers perceive the value of what they buy from you.

If I am going to do business with you today, I want your product to be of good quality. However, if I have problems with it, can I trust that you will stand behind it and make it right? This trust is becoming an important issue. It is the thing missing from many customer/brand relationships. In the New Value Equation, customer service means more than a surface level of polite behavior. It means a deep and ongoing commitment to making me, the customer, happy, today and going forward.

Customer service must be more than just the way an employee treats a customer. A customer service orientation must be integral to the overall functioning of the brand. Customers expect the way in which they are treated to be the outgrowth of a mindful, specific process. They expect brands to care deeply about customer service and to make it part of their corporate culture. Brands that understand this are JetBlue, which created JetBlue Airways' Customer Bill of Rights to "bring humanity back to air travel," and Zappos, which created its "Culture Book" to convey to employees its expectations regarding customer service. Both brands acknowledge in their actions that customer service is more than service with a smile. It's a core value of the company and a key factor that customers will weigh when choosing a brand.

How did customer service come to be a trust issue? To understand this, go back to the pervasive emotional undercurrent of today's consumer. Today's consumer is in a crisis of anxiety. What do you want when you feel anxious? You want reassurance. This is where customer service plays a critical role. Customers want companies that show empathy and humanity in their interactions with them.

Humanity is a complex combination of elements. There are many definitions of this "human face" that our customer expects to see from brands and companies.

- Quality products at competitive prices

- Fair treatment of employees

- Great customer service

- Products that are safe and reliable

- Does something for sustainability

- Giving back to the community

When we look at the New Value Equation and see customer service, we cannot simply check that off by training employees to greet customers at the door or even to be knowledgeable and helpful. The bar has been raised here, propelled by the deep and pervasive anxiety that consumers feel today. When we say customer service, we mean trust, and trust is not created in an action on the sales floor. It is an ecosystem the company must create around the product to give the consumer that sense of security.

A good example of this new customer service in action comes from Zappos. Zappos delivers on the full spectrum of New Value Equation demands, but one that stands out is its devotion to this higher level of trust-infused customer service. For Zappos, customer service is not about saying, "Have a nice day." Indeed, since the transactions are virtual, there might never be a human in the transaction at all. Yet Zappos gets top marks from consumers for customer service. Why? It surrounds the customer with company policies that reinforce over and over again: "You can trust me. I stand behind the products we sell." Take, for example, the company's shipping policy. Zappos offers free shipping in either direction. This gives the customer confidence knowing that whether she likes the shoes or hates the shoes, Zappos will cover the cost of transportation, whether she's receiving them or returning them. The willingness to cover the cost of returns is also a subtle signal of confidence to the customer: we are so sure you'll love these shoes that we'll pay for it if you want to send them back.

Zappos customer service goes beyond its free shipping policy. One of its hallmarks is the availability of its staff via digital platforms such as Twitter. Again, this goes to the heart of the customer service/ trust expectation embedded in the New Value Equation. Zappos staffers do not disappear after they've taken your money. They are still with you, still connected to you, still available to you.

Added-Value Offers

In the old days, when you opened a bank account, you could expect a free gift. Perhaps it was a toaster or some other low-level household appliance. It was never very expensive or personal, and it was accepted by all in the transaction as a token gift.

Today, in the New Value Equation, the token gift has evolved to take on significant meaning and importance. Far from being a quaint afterthought, it is a key element in the consumer's decision-making process and can sway a choice between two brands. Added value is not an add-on at all. It is an expectation. In addition to what I'm buying, what else can you give me to make me believe I'm getting more than what I'm paying for?

Many of the old freebies still speak to the modern consumer. For example, "free gift with purchase" is still appealing. When you buy a John Deere tractor, you get a free trailer. When you buy an iPhone, you get access to thousands of free apps. When you buy a GM car, you get free OnStar service for a year. The key is to be sure that the gifts are relevant and appealing to the customer and related to the initial purchase itself. The value add has to feel meaningful, not simply tacked on, to impress the customer.

Perhaps one of the most innovative ways to add value is what Hyundai did with its Assurance program. Hyundai took a risk and demonstrated to its consumers that it was willing to put something of value on the line. In the event that a customer purchased a car from Hyundai and later was laid off, Hyundai would buy back the car with no penalty. At a time when layoffs were an everyday event, this stood out as a courageous move. Hyundai offered the consumer one more powerful reason to trust its brand. The promotion set Hyundai apart by acknowledging the hard times most consumers were experiencing and showing a willingness to help bear the burden. This is a different way to add value to the purchase process.

When all these elements come together, the power of the New Value Equation becomes clear. Here is an example from my own experience. I recently purchased a new car, except that it is not new. It is certified pre-owned. If you had asked me several years ago whether I would consider buying a used car, I would have said no. I was not a used-car customer; I was a new-car customer. But my thinking about how much I pay for my transportation has evolved very much in the model of the New Value Equation. Now, I think: Why would I pay $75,000 for a vehicle that will be worth $50,000 as soon as I drive it off the lot? Why would I do that? Especially now that I can find a vehicle—one that was recently leased and is now available for sale— that meets all my quality standards?

I am comfortable that I am getting quality in my transaction. I am buying this certified pre-owned car from the same dealership that has sold me new cars over the years. I know that this is a business I can trust, one that will stand behind its products, one that will do right by me as a customer. I also know that the certified pre-owned car I drive away will not appear any different to me or my passengers than a brand new car. In the days after I made my purchase, I used the car to shuttle clients around on a fact-finding tour. Nobody realized the car they were in was not brand new. And finally, in this transaction, I was able to get a value-added offer. When negotiating at the dealership, I was offered some standard add–ons: free floor mats, license plate holders, etc. But these did not especially appeal to me. So I presented my case to the dealer. I told him I didn't want the floor mats or license plate covers, but I did want the "ding protection plan," the $900 insurance coverage against minor body damage to the vehicle. He agreed. We signed the deal. I did not get the lowest price on my vehicle. I expect someone somewhere would be willing to sell me a certified pre-owned 2008 BMW for less. But that was not my only concern. I came into the dealership wanting the product features of a BMW. I wanted quality, I wanted customer service, and I wanted value added. I got all those things, and so I was then ready to make the mental adjustment not to focus on the lowest price but to accept the competitive price because all my other needs were being met. I drove away happy.

Bringing the New Value Equation to Life

If we need the New Value Equation to entice a customer into this initial transaction with us, how do we make that happen? In previous economic cycles, the imperative to marketeers might well have been to simply pump up the volume. Spend more for advertising and marketing, increase your reach and frequency, strive to create a bigger, louder, more omnipresent footprint in the mind of the target consumer. In today's environment, that strategy is doomed to failure. It is prohibitively expensive for most companies, and furthermore, it might only serve to alienate the very consumer you hope to attract. Today's smart and savvy consumer does not want to be on the receiving end of a hard sell. Quite the opposite. The greatest joy in consumer activity comes in the act of discovery—uncovering something relevant and unique and appealing. To bring the New Value Equation to life for your brand, you need to find ways to let the consumer discover your value.

Case Study: Walmart

Having examined the New Value Equation and its role in getting consumers to that all-important first transaction, now we take a closer look at a company that has pulled this all together: Walmart.

Walmart presents a powerful case study for the New Value Equation, in part because it was so rooted in its early years in the old one.

The company that Sam Walton founded and built was 100 percent committed to the old value equation. The slogan said it clearly: "Always low prices. Always." In fact, that's even a softening of what Sam Walton himself wanted to say in the slogan. As the company grew into a Wall Street darling, Sam Walton, a product of a Depression Era upbringing, wanted to continue his traditional slogan of "Always the low price. Always." This underscored his belief that *the* lowest price was his primary reason for being in business. But his lawyers intervened and convinced him that promising *the* lowest price could open him up to legal trouble. He relented and "Always Low Prices. Always." was born.

Yet as the world changed around Walmart, the slogan—and the devotion to low price as a strategy—began to lose steam. Walmart found itself losing market share to companies like Target, which promoted a new marketing message, one steeped in the savvy shopper outlook of the New Value Equation. Walmart could no longer rely on its old standby to move it forward in the post-9/11, post–Great Recession economy. Sam Walton was gone, and it was time for his focus on price, and the old value equation, to go, too.

Walmart embraced the elements of the New Value Equation with determination. It put resources into new news, creating and promoting new partnerships like the one with Apple to sell the iPhone. It promoted a new emphasis on food, not always considered a core Walmart product. It reworked its marketing messages to acknowledge "real" family and reflect an image to customers that they could relate to. The giant corporate conglomerate worked hard to show more of a human face, becoming more involved in political activism and eco-conscious programs. And through all this, the company was able to maintain a sense of nostalgia by retaining its traditional front-door greeters.

The final migration from old value equation to New Value Equation came in the logo and slogan. "Save money. Live better." showed the evolution of the Walmart brand position and the company's clarified understanding of the consumer mindset. Consumers were no longer hyper-focused on price, as perhaps the late Sam Walton had remembered them. They were looking for a more broad definition of value, one that saved them money but also improved their lives. Both were equally important to the consumer, and the new logo communicated that they were equally important to Walmart as well.

Sam Walton, always concerned about putting his customer first, would surely approve.

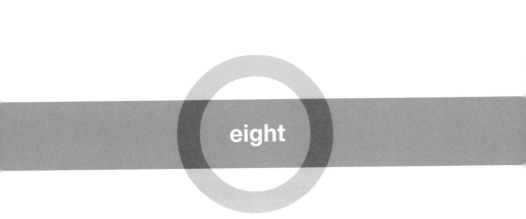

eight

Magnifying Consumer Attraction to Your Brand

If you followed the principles in the last chapter and delivered a New Value Equation to your prospects, you got the first transaction from them. You added a new customer to your franchise. You acquired a new name in your database. Congratulations! Now what?

Most *marketers* at this time believe that their job is done and they move on to finding new prospects. The job of keeping the new customer that they just acquired is now in the hands of some other people in some other department. *Marketeers* know better. They know that they need to move these new customers up the pathway toward a brand ritual.

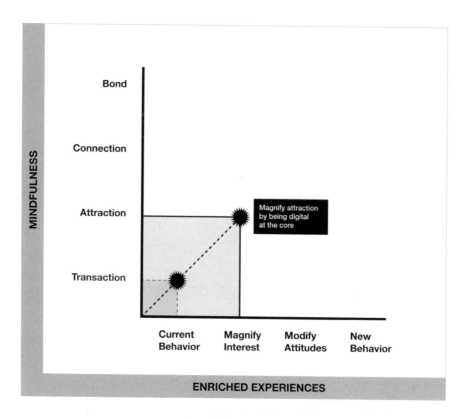

To do this, you need to take this first transaction and create conditions to make this behavior happen consistently. You need to get frequency. You need to increase the attraction that your new customer feels for your brand in a way that magnifies interest in your brand. The question then is:

How do you move from "I just met you" to "I like you"?

We often find ourselves in this position having made an initial connection, be it business or personal. We want very much to move the relationship forward. Still, somehow, we struggle to gain any kind of momentum. Most times the forward motion never takes hold, and our connection sputters and fizzles. This is why traditional marketers stay in a constant state of acquisition marketing.

The parallels between the business and the personal are striking. Think for a moment about the way a romantic relationship might progress. Let's say you're a man who meets a woman and wants to get to know her better. You invite her on a date. She agrees to go to dinner and a movie with you. You are on your way!

The date goes well. What is your next step? Do you do the same thing again? Another dinner and a movie? It worked once, right? Why not again?

If your answer is "Wait and see what happens" or "Do the same thing all over again," then you can imagine where this budding romance might go! Without showing a positive response to her and some initiative, your first date might well be your *only* date.

The same is true in a brand relationship. If your efforts produced a "first date" or initial transaction, well done. You've got a good start. But if you do not use that first transaction as a platform for more and better interactions, your connection might simply fade. In a romantic situation, you want to build on the first date. If she mentioned that she liked a certain kind of music, you might get tickets for a concert. If she talked about art or dancing, you might plan an outing to a gallery opening or dance club. If she told you she can't stand flowers, you would send chocolate. This shows you heard what she said and want to please her—which helps to magnify and deepen your relationship. Then you would move from an initial date into a period of courtship.

A brand relationship is just like dating. You must capitalize on your success in securing the initial transaction with efforts to woo the consumer and magnify his or her attraction to your brand. That might be good or bad news for you, depending upon the status of your love life . . . but at the very least, the parallels provide some instruction for the marketeer.

Become Digital at the Core

Unlike love, creating a deeper interest in your brand is not mystical and hard to fathom. You don't need to understand "what a woman really wants" or "what will get a man to call for a next date." Indeed, given the advent of digital technology—the penetration of the internet and mobility—there have never been so many ways for a marketeer to magnify consumer interest in a brand as there are today. The digital ecosystem creates a tremendous number of possibilities (sometimes too many). The trick is to deploy these tools and approaches with care and precision.

The most important action that brands need to take to magnify attraction is to become digital at their core. When I say this, I am not suggesting that you do another e-mail campaign, execute a display campaign, do a big search campaign, deepen your Facebook presence, send tweets, become active on foursquare, do promotions on Groupon, or build a mobile app. These are all examples of digital marketing tactics, and all good ones that might well give your brand a boost. What I am suggesting is much broader and much more strategic.

My advice to you is not simply to get enamored by all the digital tools and tactics, but to look at how your brand can integrate the digital opportunity at the core of its strategic value proposition. This is a philosophical state of *mind*, not just a tactical state of *being*. To make this a successful journey, your brand must find this inner digital ethos—or risk appearing shallow and out-of-touch with the current consumer expectations.

Why is this so critical? The digital world we live in today enables us to deliver engaging and credible experiences to our customers that bring the brand value proposition to life in a real, meaningful way. These experiences have the ability to create differentiated brand positions. This is especially true in our society, where the digital environment has taken control from the digital purveyors and placed it into the hands of the consumer. Yes. Yours and mine. *Time* magazine got this. Its January 1, 2006, issue named its person of the year "You." That's what the magazine cover read. That single word was depicted on a then state-of-the-art PC screen.

The text went on to explain that the world had entered the information age and that this era would be characterized and driven by the technology-enabled individual consumer. "You control the Information Age," *Time* declared to its readers. "Welcome to your world."

It is in this world, the space of the digitally empowered individual consumer, that your brand must live and thrive. To appeal to this digital consumer, a brand must also be digital, and not just in its tactics but in its soul. That's what I mean by digital at the core.

That feels like a big statement. It is an important one. It is simply recognition of what has happened to the world around us. We have moved from a society that used technology to enable better productivity, connections, and relationships to one that is deeply intertwined with technology at every minute of the day. It has become the basis of all our activities. Ironic how quickly things have changed.

Just a few short years ago, it was possible to separate consumers into those who shopped online and those who did not. Today, that distinction doesn't really exist. The digital world has encroached on every aspect of the shopping experience.

There might be those consumers out there who do not transact digitally, but that does not mean they do not shop online. Consumers are intimately involved with the online world as they shop and buy. Perhaps in the mid-nineties, it was the true "early adopter" who would use his or her computer to research a product before buying it. Now, that first online search is a basic part of shopping. If I am looking for a new flat-screen TV, my first stop is my computer. I might let my favorite search engines lead me to sites that give me more information. I might start out with the websites of my favorite stores. Or I might begin with a consumer-oriented site that aggregates the content that will inform my decision. I will scroll through the comments section for consumer opinions. I will spend time on sites like Yelp to get other reviews. I will share and discuss my choices on Facebook. The idea that I would decide to buy a TV and just head out to the store to get it without going online first is almost funny. Who would do that? In today's world, that would be a sign of a poorly informed consumer.

Most marketeers recognize this "digital normalcy." The question is, what do we do about it? Meet your customer in this environment and magnify their attraction to your brand.

When it comes to this, perhaps no other toolbox is more attractive to marketeers than that offered by social channels. Social media—Facebook, Twitter, YouTube, foursquare, and those yet to be invented—are fueling tremendous discussion in marketing circles. They are not just tactics. They are platforms. They don't simply drive transactions. They create environments to help consumers learn more about a product or service and drive a deeper engagement with the brand. When it comes time to demonstrate that a brand is digital to the core, often the best place to do that is in a social media environment.

Take Blendtec, for example. Here is a brand that leveraged the digital space to create a huge following and build its business.

What's so interesting about a blender? It sits on your countertop. It crushes ice for your party drinks, maybe garlic for your pesto sauce. It is not an item that most consumers devote a lot of time or attention to purchasing or using. That presents a significant challenge to a company hoping to create a brand ritual using the lowly blender. How can you create brand attraction in a product that is so familiar and domestic?

Blendtec approached this challenge by launching the Will It Blend? campaign on YouTube. Web videos featured company president Tom Dickson putting the Blendtec products through their paces in a series of escalating experiments. In each video short, Dickson picked an object—a lightbulb, a golf club, even an iPod—and asked the question: will it blend? The object was then dropped into the Blendtec and pulverized before the virtual eyes of the YouTube audience.

The campaign was a hit. Not only did Blendtec raise its brand awareness with core customers (commercial users such as smoothie shops), home sales of its blenders soared 700 percent. Why?

Something about human nature makes us gravitate toward destruction in progress. We stand and watch as old stadiums are dynamited to dust. We chase tornadoes. We tune in eagerly to television shows that crush, crumble, and crunch objects and actors alike. We can't help but look. Will It Blend? picks up on this pleasure we take in watching the destructive process—particularly in this format where no living beings were at risk. It was an acceptable way to enjoy destruction of different items.

The video shorts did more than get our attention: they successfully demonstrated the prowess of the product. You want to crush ice? This baby will make ice crushing look like child's play. The entertainment aspect of the videos was inextricably bound up in the successful operation of the machine. Every blending challenge was another opportunity for Blendtec to show off exactly what it does so well. The relevance connection was strong and obvious to all.

They were digital at the core. Blendtec made the first step by distributing its marketing message via YouTube. It then went further, embracing several key elements of digital lifestyle. It encouraged interactivity: viewers could send in suggestions for what Tom should blend next. It created a separate website (willitblend.com), which featured both the extraordinary exploits of the blender that could only be conducted safely in a lab as well as "blend it at home" projects the viewer could safely try. The combination of the online format and interactivity gave this program its digital core attributes.

Two Key Principles

I want to pause for an important discussion around two key principles to develop compelling digital experiences. The question you need to ask yourself: is this interesting *and* relevant?

Far too many marketers stop at just "interesting" and fail to consider "relevant" for their digital programs. This breakdown is where many potential brand relationships are lost.

Because the digital and social environments offer us many tools and techniques, this might seem like a candy store of possibilities. But it is critical not to be seduced by what is *possible* in the digital environment and to remain focused on what your customer will consider *organic* to his or her experience. Simply put, a unique message delivered digitally will be well received only if it is considered relevant. If it is not relevant to the consumer, the message will not only be ineffective, it might be considered an insult. ("How dare this company send me spam! I am offended, and I am unsubscribing this instant.")

Go back to the dating world. On your first night out, your date expresses a love of flowers. The next day, you send chocolate. Now you have dug yourself a hole. You have demonstrated that you were not listening. Just communicating the next day is not enough. You need to communicate in a way that is relevant to the recipient. Picture your date opening the box of chocolates and saying to her girlfriends, "I spent half of last night telling him how much I love flowers. Didn't he listen to a word I was saying?"

A marketeer can inspire this same reaction in a customer by sending an irrelevant communication. Too often, traditional marketing thinking results in the company simply sending the next promotion on the calendar to a new customer, without regard to whether that person will find it relevant. This is roulette. Perhaps the customer will like the communication; perhaps she will consider it spam. Is that a gamble you want to take with your brand? *Well over 90 percent of traditional marketers make the fundamental mistake of sending irrelevant communication.*

To be sure, determining relevance is not easy. You need to have data on your consumer. You need to have the will and the expertise to not only collect that data but also analyze it and extract useful information from it. You have to be willing to take what the customer has *said* and determine what the customer *means*. This is not simple work, but it is critical.

Simply being "interesting" is not enough. Relevance is key. Blendtec did both. It made its demos interesting, but, by using difficult-to-blend stuff, it was also able to communicate clearly the high-performance capability of its blenders.

Another example of relevance is how Hotmail was launched. Let's go back to the year 1996 and see how the marketeers at Hotmail targeted relevant prospects in the digital environment. I do believe that this was one of the very first viral marketing campaigns executed online. Hotmail came on the scene with little fanfare—an internet startup back when such things were as common as mosquitoes in the summer in Chicago. Its fundamental challenge was to find a way to create brand attraction for Hotmail, an e-mail service on a shoestring budget going up against the category leader in AOL and a strong contender in Yahoo!

The campaign was simple and genius. It consisted of one line of hyperlinked text that appeared in every Hotmail e-mail sent. It read, "Get your free e-mail at Hotmail!" and linked back to Hotmail's website for more information. No other explanation, promotion, or exhortation. Turns out, none was necessary. That one little line, embedded in every user's e-mails, spread the word. Less than six months post-launch, Hotmail had one million users. At the eighteen-month mark, it had almost twelve million. No subscriber-based media product had ever grown so big so quickly.

Perhaps today, when we are so used to commercial messages infiltrating our e-mail, we might not have noticed something as small and subtle as the Hotmail invitation. But in 1996, including a commercial tagline in an ordinary e-mail was a paradigm shift. The communication system of e-mail had not yet been used effectively in this manner. The audacity of the effort was interest-generating in and of itself. What's more, the Hotmail offer was notable in what it did *not* do. It did not shout or overpromise or attempt to seem larger than life. It was interesting in its simplicity. Within the ecosystem of the breathlessly promotional dot-com era, the direct approach of Hotmail's offer set the company and the campaign apart.

It also focused on the right customers. Who wants to know about innovations in e-mail service? Why, e-mail users, of course. The Hotmail campaign scored a bull's-eye in this regard. Anyone who saw the campaign was, without a doubt, an e-mail user. Information pertaining to an e-mail service was therefore 100 percent relevant to the reader. Few marketing campaigns hit their targets with such accuracy. This helped them connect with their constituents in a meaningful way by providing them the content to forward to their friends and contacts.

By doing it this way, Hotmail was true to its digital heritage. It used e-mail as its primary transmission tool, and it harnessed users to spread the word to potential customers (long before the term "user-generated content" was coined). Furthermore, this campaign was the heart of the Hotmail launch strategy. It was not an extra to be tacked on to the end of a print and television blitz. Hotmail was a brand that would live by its ability to be digital at its core. It became a leading player. Microsoft acquired it in December 1997 to be an integral offering of the MSN Network. Although financial terms of the deal weren't disclosed, it was a stock-swap transaction; one industry executive speculated that the value of the deal was as high as $400 million.

If you've been tracking with these examples, you might be wondering, Can this work for categories like consumer packaged goods or fast food or event services? Every category has examples of how successful brands are executing programs that are organic and conceived to be digital. The Isaiah Mustafa campaign by Old Spice ("The Man Your Man Could Smell Like") is one of my favorites. Using him as a spokesperson and creating more than 180 videos to respond to customer requests and interests was a very effective way to take a personal care brand and make it interesting and relevant to its group. Based on market data, it definitely seems to have increased the level of attraction for the brand among its customer group.

Another example that I think does a terrific job is one created by the French office of Euro RSCG (my old employer) for Evian.

As you might know, Evian is a mature brand, owned by global food company Danone. Like a number of mature packaged goods brands, Evian was in a slow-growth mode in a very competitive market that looked to be getting commoditized and homogenized. There was no immediate crisis: Evian was the market leader. It was holding its own. Consumers were not jumping ship. But there was no sense of fun or excitement in the brand. It had developed a bit of a stale, uninspiring persona. This had to change.

Evian launched a new campaign with the theme "Live Young." As part of this, the agency developed a one-minute video short originally aired via the newly developed "digital out of home" platform—namely TV screens in retail stores. But what started as a store-based experience soon moved to personal computer screens, and in this digital environment, a phenomenon was born. "Live Young" soon became known as "Roller Babies." The video used computer-generated animation to depict babies on roller skates, rocking out in an urban park to the tune of "Rapper's Delight."

The campaign literally made history. It appears in *The Guinness Book of World Records* as the most-viewed online ad in history, tallying more than sixty million viewers and more than fifty-four thousand comments via Twitter and other social networking platforms.

This is the kind of campaign consumers seek out for the entertainment value alone. This is interesting. The use of technology to show babies break dancing, back flipping, and busting moves around Evian water bottles kept the laughs rolling. Precocious babies have long been a source of entertainment in movies (*Look Who's Talking*), television (*Family Guy*), and advertising (E★Trade). Evian successfully tapped this vein to draw consumer interest.

Evian had something in common with its target customer: both were staring down the barrel of middle age. Evian's target audience was aged twenty-four to forty-nine, with $75,000-plus annual income. It was an audience of grown-ups. And sometimes grown-ups feel restless, even when they've become so accomplished. They wish they could recapture the joy of their youth. Evian, too, was concerned it had become a grown-up (and not joyous) brand. Sharing that mindset created relevancy for the ad campaign. Evian was reasserting its ability to be youthful and fun and outrageous and invited its grown-up customers to seize the moment and do the same.

Evian made two essential moves in asserting its digital soul through this campaign. The first was in creating the content, and the second was in distributing it. To create the ad, Evian tapped the digital toolbox. The babies were not animated, they were computer generated. The underlying technical expertise was part of the entertainment factor. Second, the one-minute video was not broadcast on TV or as a screen-grab for print. It made its way around the world via YouTube, driven by viewers who saw it, loved it, and shared it with friends. The pass-along quality of the campaign's distribution gave it digital credibility that a broadcast media run could not have equaled. It also helped the brand improve its share in a number of key markets around the world.

These are some examples of how brands can leverage their digital ethos to increase the attraction their customers feel by creating interesting content that delivers on a relevant need or connects with a relevant truth to engage and inspire their customers.

A Construct for the Programs

Having met your customer in his or her digital habitat, what is your next move? To create attraction, you need an appealing invitation. You want to ask your customer to join you in something special, something unique and appealing and relevant—so you can get beyond that first date. This brings us to the discussion of the insider deal.

Consumers *love* this concept! These are the backstage passes of the consumer experience, making us feel special and valued. Offering your customer insider status is a critical step in creating attraction. Look at the process again through the dating prism. If you want to get the girl to go out with you again, do you offer her an experience that anyone can have? Or do you work to create one that she will see immediately is special and something that only she, as the chosen individual, will receive? And once she feels special, that will influence her feelings about you. The same is true in the brand relationship. The more you can convince your consumer that he or she is getting an insider deal, the more special and valued that consumer will feel.

This also ties back to a key element in the New Value Equation, and that is the mindset of the "smart" shopper. Over the years, as the value equation has evolved, consumers have begun to prize their own brainpower in the process. They do not stand around, waiting patiently in the hopes something good will come along. They seek a good deal. They seek relevant information. They seek the opinions of others. All of this effort is expended because they don't just want to acquire an *item*. They want to *feel smart* about acquiring that item. Part of the joy of shopping is not just getting a product but getting a good deal. Knowing that, the role of the insider offer becomes even more relevant in creating attraction to your brand. When the consumer can get a good deal, she not only feels special, she also feels smart. She has made choices that led her to this special offer. She feels good about herself, and she feels good about you.

The insider deal is tailor-made for the digital age. If you offer a deal by taking out a print ad or running a TV spot, how special is that? Not very. Mass advertising is a terrible medium for any kind of insider information. If millions can get the message, the experience is not all that special.

Digital communication, on the other hand, is perfectly suited for the kind of targeted connection that makes the recipient feel unique. It might be an e-mail sent to a single address. It might be a website accessible only by password. It might be a text message received only by the "followers" of a specific poster. This information comes across as decidedly insider. Only the chosen few will learn about it. This elevates the communication, making it more special than other advertising or marketing messages your consumer might receive that day.

As an example, Restoration Hardware makes use of the digital world to offer select consumers an insider experience. As all retailers do, the company holds regular sales. These are events designed to spur activity, perhaps move some aging inventory out the door. But instead of tossing up a "Sale!" sign, Restoration Hardware offers a select group of online users early access to the discounted merchandise. Consumers receive an e-mail inviting them to experience the sale first before it is opened to the public.

Starbucks also marries the use of digital communication and insider access. As part of its revival strategy, the coffee company began offering a series of specialty "small batch" coffees. But not everyone got the news of the new coffees at once. Instead, first dibs went out via e-mail to a select group of customers.

This is the backstage tour. The consumer has been singled out as special and then offered a deal. To be sure, eventually everyone will be able to visit Restoration Hardware and shop at the sale. Ultimately, Starbucks will sell any coffee in its warehouse to anyone who wants it.

But in both these cases, the marketeers used their digital understanding to create a moment of special connection with their customers as a way to deepen their attraction with the brand.

Everyone likes to feel acknowledged and rewarded, and consumers especially want to feel smart. The insider deal is a great way to achieve that mindset. Being digital at the core can help make the offerings possible.

Create a Value-Added Interaction

What else can you do? Remember that your goal in this process is not simply to check off the steps but to improve on the relationship and magnify attraction for your brand. After recognizing the digital reality of your customer and offering insider access using digital tools, consider what else you can give to make the deal even sweeter.

Going back again to the New Value Equation, this is an opportunity to offer an extra. Look for ways a promotion can provide more than a come-on. Imbue digital promotions with a sense of added value for the consumer. When they answer a survey, enter them into a sweepstakes. When they make a purchase, reward them with a prize. When I make a purchase, naturally my first goal is to acquire the item I desire at a competitive price. When I am also offered an extra, that further cements my relationship to the brand and gives me another opportunity to feel good about myself as a shopper and about the brand.

This is an experience I have had many times as a customer of Jos. A. Bank. I came to the brand attracted by its combination of style, quality, and competitive price. Those factors were enough to encourage me into an initial transaction. But I am now a loyal customer in part because the brand routinely goes the extra step and offers me something additional. Sometimes it will be a matching tie. Sometimes it will be an early heads up on an upcoming sale. Sometimes it will be a discount on an additional purchase. But always, the concept of the extra is present in my dealings with this company. By following this behavior, the brand does more than satisfy my need for a new suit. It feeds my desire to have an extra that makes me feel as though I have made a smart retail choice.

The extra is an important part of the New Value Equation, and the digital environment is an excellent platform for delivering this.

I hope you will see that by beginning to use your digital ethos, you as a marketeer have the ability to move the customer from the first transaction to building a level of attraction with your brand. It is our job to make use of the new digital landscape, embrace the digital lifestyle that already envelops the consumer, and use it to magnify the consumer's attraction to what we offer as the second step in moving closer to our goal of creating a brand ritual.

nine

Building Connections with Relevant Innovations and Experiences

Pity the poor, unappreciated existing customer. That's me. That's you. That's all of us.

Consider the individual who has made a purchase—maybe many purchases—but gets no love from the brand. It's as though by purchasing your product, he's become invisible. All the exciting promotions, all the new ideas and innovation the company has to offer spill freely into the marketplace in search of new customers. But that is all specially designed to attract newcomers. If the existing customer tries to get in on those discounts or that free gift, he is likely to be told, "Sorry, no. That promotion is not available to you. It is only for new customers."

It's enough to make a loyal customer disloyal. Or definitely very angry. In all my years talking to customers in research, this is the one behavior of brands they cannot understand. "How can you treat someone who has been spending money with you like this?" they ask.

Crazy as it might sound, this type of brush-off happens all the time. Telecommunications companies are famous for it. When you see an ad for a great new deal on cell phone service, let your eyes drift down to the small print at the bottom. Chances are excellent that deal is offered only to new customers. If you are already a customer of this brand, too bad for you! You are stuck with your old deal. The same is true for cable companies. For insurance companies. I am sure you can add a lot more categories to this list. These are the categories where consumers feel like they're held hostage by the brands. They're also the ones with the smallest group of "loyal" or "bonded" customers.

My favorite personal example is Comcast. We moved into a new house. Our only choice for cable was Comcast. With no other choice, I signed up for its top-of-the-line service, Triple Play. With this I get all cable channels, high-speed internet, and telephone service. About forty-five days after I signed up, I saw a new campaign from Xfinity (I know it is Comcast but still haven't figured out what this is) for the same package at 20 percent less than what I had just begun to pay. So, I called Comcast, and after being on hold for about an hour, I find out from the representative that I do not qualify for this deal . . . "Sir, you are already a customer." I'm not very happy. Every month when I see my bill, I am unhappier.

For most of us that have been in the business for a while, this state of affairs is not surprising. Even today, most CMOs' objectives are to drive new traffic, new customer acquisition, and net new revenue. New, new, new. It is all about acquisition marketing. Most of the marketing budgets are for new acquisition marketing. Ironic, given the fact that if you look at the economics of the business, a large percentage of its profits comes from a relatively small number of core (what some might consider loyal) customers.

For two decades now, research has told us that acquiring new customers is far more expensive than retaining current customers.

Yet we are constantly chasing these new accounts. Why? Perhaps it is the thrill of the hunt. Perhaps it's the fantasy of the undiscovered country. But whatever the reason, it is a danger to you and your brand. The process of searching for new customers is expensive, time consuming, and distracting from the more important work you should be pursuing. The real goal should be much closer to home: in your own databases, on your own customer rosters. This is the group that will move you into brand ritual status if you are just willing to put in the work and not become distracted by customers you've yet to meet. If you focus on them, you will be able to drive better economic returns for your business.

In stage three, we will look at this critical juncture in the ritual-building process. This is the point where many traditional marketeers disengage and let the rest of the business (mostly operations) take the lead. Which is unfortunate, as this is the point where, after getting your first transaction and magnifying their attraction to your brand (the customer has agreed to come back to do business with your brand, perhaps many times), you find yourselves in a place where an existing customer hangs in the balance between deepening his engagement with your brand and flirting with your competitors. What will happen next? Will he move further along in his relationship with your brand?

This stage in the process has tremendous potential for the marketeer. This is the point where the customer is not just making a short-term decision but establishing a mindful, long-term connection to your brand. The customer is ready to place your brand at the heart of the decision-making process. This is the type of customer who thinks, "I want a Starbucks" rather than "I want a coffee" or says, "I'm going to Google it" rather than "I'm going to do an internet search." The brand is making itself part of the customer thinking. This is where so much of your work as a marketeer is starting to pay off.

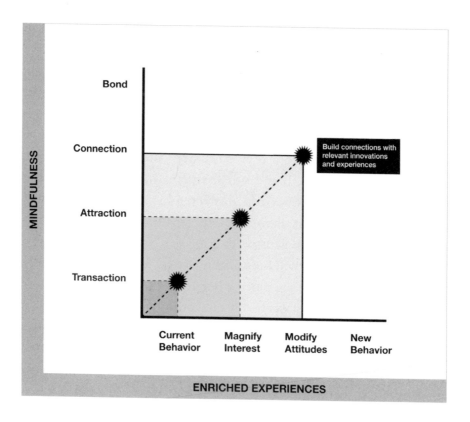

Build Connections
with Relevant Innovations and Experiences

There has been a trend lately (again) for brands to consider building loyalty programs as a way to keep current customers engaged with their brands. I have written about this many times on my blog. I tend to believe that not every brand needs a loyalty program. Most just need a frequency marketing program to make using the brand a habit for their customers. By becoming a regular part of their lives, the brand will move on to become a routine and then establish a basis for connection. However, among the marketing community, there is a lot of momentum toward building loyalty programs. Every marketer wants to model its program after companies like Tesco, Kroger, Harrah's, and Best Buy, to name a few. They believe that by building these types of loyalty programs, they can build the appropriate connections and keep customers in their franchise.

I beg to disagree. I am a fan of loyalty programs, but only if these programs are developed based on a broader business context to help deliver meaningful innovations that add value to the customer. These innovations should make them believe that your brand understands them and has the ability to fulfill their needs in a manner that none of your competitors can.

Learn from your existing customer base. Use behavioral data from their experiences with your brand and category to obtain deep insights on how you can serve their needs in new, interesting, and relevant ways. Don't expect the data to come forward with this insight. Learn to extract it. Start with hypotheses and then dig deep. The best and most actionable insights come when you find the balance between what your customers do and what they say. Most times, there is a level of dissonance there. Understanding the reasons for this dissonance can provide big ideas, which can result in innovations that serve the needs of your customers better than any of your competitors. These innovations can then deepen their connection with your brand. And bring them one step closer to becoming part of a brand ritual.

Over the next few pages, I want to share stories from some of the brands that have developed deep connections with their customers.

Tesco: Customized Clubs Make Customers Feel Understood and Special

Retail giant Tesco provides a fascinating and instructive case of how it has consistently leveraged its knowledge and insights into customers to deliver meaningful and differentiated innovations. By deepening its connections with customers, Tesco has hastened more of them down a path toward brand ritual and in the process transformed its own business.

A bit of history: In the mid-1990s, Tesco was not on anyone's radar screen. It was the No. 3 grocery chain in the UK. It sold only food. It had no global aspirations. It had no e-commerce presence. It was the very picture of a brand in neutral. Customers who might have been enticed by a sale or a convenient location were given no reason to stay and bond with this retailer.

Then Tesco made a key move. It decided to say "thank you." It launched a rather ordinary-sounding program called Clubcard that allowed Tesco customers to earn points on their purchases. They could then redeem their points for discounts on future purchases. The loyalty program itself was not all that innovative—lots of retailers had programs just like Clubcard. It's what Tesco did next that redrew the retail map.

Tesco began mining the data from its Clubcard customers and using that information to design innovations in products and services. Some of the early incarnations were quite basic. Noticing a trend in baby products, Tesco rolled out Baby Club. Its members were offered coupons, magazines and newsletters, contests, and even a special permit that allowed them to park in spots close to the store. From Baby Club, it was not a big stretch to also roll out Toddler Club and Kids Club, recognizing that in the inexorable march of time, these customers were all one. These programs were designed to show customers that Tesco was listening and responding to their needs.

Baby Club and its siblings were just the tip of the iceberg. Tesco began developing all manner of specialty collectives based on the spending habits of its customers. Clubs to serve wine enthusiasts, healthy living devotees, foodies, and frequent travelers all sprung up. At each juncture, Tesco read the tea leaves of its Clubcard databases and came up with ways to enrich the lives of its most loyal customers. This was not a pitch to new customers. It was an ongoing thank you to existing ones.

Why is something as simple as a club significant to consumers? Certainly everyone likes rewards points. But there is another current running through this process that does more than reward the customer—it builds a connection between the customer and the brand. Tesco, by forming these clubs, is communicating to its customers that it understands their specific needs and is responding to these with relevant offerings that add value to their relationship with the brand.

This is a compelling message. If I am going to spend my hard-earned money, I need to make a choice about which retailer to visit. The idea that a store understands me—my life, my challenges, and the experiences I have every day—is a powerful draw. It recalls the relationships that shoppers once had with independent local grocers. These shop owners knew everyone in the neighborhood. They could tell you who had just had a baby, whose son was graduating from high school, and who had just became a grandma. Tesco, by tapping into its databases, re-creates that corner store operator for the modern age. Tesco can't know each of its customers by sight, but it can know a lot about its customers as a group and tailor innovations to their lives. In a world where we often feel anonymous, the act of showing the customer you know what he or she is going through is powerful.

Tesco's innovations aren't limited to services and discounts. The company has also introduced new or improved products when it saw an unfilled need. For example, drawing on information gleaned from its World of Wine club, it gave all Tesco-branded wines a screw–cap design, rolled out new lighter-weight bottles and unveiled the Zork, a resealable top for sparkling wine. Tesco described all three changes as ways to "revolutionise the wine industry and help customers"—existing customers, as it did in developing the clubs, not just new customers.

As customers responded, Tesco took the effort further. Innovation was not restricted to the company's R&D departments: all staffers were encouraged to share their best ideas. Thousands came in every year. Tesco ran contests to encourage its vendors to be innovative in their own processes and products. It even opened its application-programming interface to third-party developers, encouraging them to come in and design apps that consumers might enjoy. Technology experts were free to develop specialized applications for niche markets, such as an app that displayed gluten-free Tesco products or one that aided the shopper in calorie counting.

All this innovation helped the company grow. In a decade, Tesco went from a domestic grocer in the UK to a global enterprise with stores in thirteen countries, a range of product lines from clothing and electronics to food and financial services, and distinction as the UK's No. 1 online retailer. The firm was transformed and found legions of new customers. But the core of the Tesco experience is its relationship with existing customers. From the start, Tesco let its customers say where and how the innovations should happen. It built a connection to its customers through innovative products and experiences.

Terry Hunt, Chairman of EHS Brann, one of the creators of the Clubcard program, said this well when he said, "What Tesco Clubcard has done is fundamentally change, not just marketing at Tesco, but the entire business." This is an important learning. A loyalty program is not the end (although a number of marketers treat it as such). It is the means to an end. The end is superior customer insight. In the case of Tesco, because the Clubcard rewards frequency and value of purchase, customers are willing to identify themselves every time they shop. By analyzing what customers do rather than what they say they do, they learned volumes about their business. Tesco couldn't have gained this breadth and depth of knowledge any other way. This is an important point I make to clients and companies: your customers and their behaviors can provide deep and meaningful insights that can drive compelling innovation to build deeper connections, all while modifying their behavior toward your brand.

Allstate: Thanking Loyal Customers in a Meaningful Way

Allstate is another example of how a century-old company in a very competitive and commoditized category used insight to deliver innovation that deepened their connection and built a broader portfolio relationship with their customers.

Allstate faced a common challenge of leadership. After years as an established, respected player in the auto insurance industry, its brand image was aging. Newer competitors, such as Geico and Progressive, were surging with their fun, engaging ad campaigns. Allstate, by contrast, appeared old and staid.

This was more than a crisis of reputation: it was a crisis of customer retention. Allstate needed to find a way to keep its customers engaged and attached to the brand so that they would not be lured away to the newer, more hip and fun competition.

Allstate turned to its employees for new ways to be more compelling to existing customers.

Inside the company, innovation became a mantra. Allstate opened a "play lab" stocked with toys and other interesting objects designed to inspire staffers to open their minds and think about innovation and customer satisfaction in new ways. Managers reported that teams would schedule brainstorming sessions in the play lab as a way to foster creative thinking.

As ideas began to flow, Allstate managers tried to evaluate and test them with as much transparency as possible, allowing staffers to see how their suggestions were being received.

Finally, executives made clear that occasional failure was an acceptable outcome. They understood that to be too careful would mean dampening the flow of innovation. Better to try, fail quickly, and try again rather than proceed with too much caution and go nowhere.

With innovation percolating throughout the company, changes began to emerge in the way Allstate treated its existing customers. It instituted programs that served as a reward system, a thank you to good customers who remained loyal. People who managed to get through a year without an accident, for example, were rewarded by seeing their deductibles go down.

Another example of an Allstate innovation came in the form of accident forgiveness. This was Allstate's acknowledgment that life happens, and sometimes even the best of drivers gets into an accident. For many people, the dismay of an accident is compounded by the knowledge that this most likely will drive up their insurance rates. Allstate could take the conventional wisdom—accident = rate hike—and turn it into a moment to show appreciation to loyal customers.

I experienced the power of this innovation myself when my family had an issue with one of our cars, a minivan, during the Christmas holidays a couple of years ago. I had taken my family to a museum. While we were enjoying the exhibit, someone broke the van window, reached in, and stole the GPS from the dashboard. Of course I was upset. My car was damaged. My family outing was marred. I would have to have the car repaired and the GPS replaced. But also, as is often the case in a mishap such as this, I dreaded the call to the insurance company.

I was pleasantly surprised when I made the call, explained my situation, and heard, "Don't worry, Mr. Raj. This won't affect your rates." Music to my ears. Now, not only am I happy that my insurance covered my loss; I am further bonded to the company because it "forgave" my claim. I was not penalized, as has often been the history of the insurance industry. Accident forgiveness deepened my connection with the brand. It has also modified my behavior. I am more willing now, given my positive experience, to consider other products such as life insurance from the company. I certainly am not feeling the need to jump ship to one of Allstate's competitors. The company showed that it values me and wants to keep me happy and in the fold. Their innovations worked.

Hyundai: Understanding and Alleviating Customers' Fears

If there is one danger in the innovation process, it is that we get so caught up in the excitement of creating something new that we lose sight of how the customer will respond to our innovation. It's a trap that technology companies often slip into when they become enamored of an invention and fail to see how the gizmo—no matter how cool it is—will not fit in with customers and their lives. This happens to brands, too.

When focused on innovation, you have to be careful not to get too caught up in the "wow" factor of newness. You must remain focused on the full mission of this stage of brand ritual development: build connections with relevant innovations and experiences. This next case study is a prime example of that relevancy at work.

Like the rest of the auto industry, Hyundai struggled mightily in 2008. As financial institutions crumbled and economies shuddered, consumers shut down. They spent as little as possible, cutting back in almost every sector, and refusing en masse to put out large sums of cash for something like an automobile unless they had to. The industry was at a standstill.

At that time, Hyundai had a marketing executive in the field conducting focus groups. Everywhere he went, he heard the same story: "You guys make a pretty good inexpensive car, but we're just not buying it. We're too worried about our jobs. Don't you get that?"

The marketing exec *did* get that. And he came up with an innovative way to address that very timely emotion. He developed the idea for the Hyundai Assurance Program. It promised the consumer a "no fault" purchase. If you buy a Hyundai and you lose your job through no fault of your own within a year of signing a purchase agreement, you can bring the vehicle back. No penalty. No black mark on your credit report.

The program was certainly innovative. What car company had ever agreed to take a vehicle back with no penalty? Indeed, the auto industry is better known for creating complicated financing deals that lure struggling consumers into burdensome loans and unfortunate meetings with the repo man. A "no fault" return policy was an entirely new idea.

At the same time, it was spot-on relevant. Focus group participants had been telling Hyundai execs about their worries, and Hyundai responded with a worry reducer. It was an emotional bull's-eye. Other brands have tapped into this vein by creating programs that alleviate the fear of buyer's remorse. We've already noted Zappos' policy of paying return shipping for its customers so that they can stop worrying about whether the shoes will fit. But it costs a lot less to take back a pair of shoes than to take back a car. The enormity of Hyundai's promise was striking. It was the seller of a big-ticket item willing to take a big-ticket risk in order to help its customers feel more secure. You could not help but feel awe at the move.

Customers responded almost immediately. The Hyundai Assurance Plan was announced in October 2008. In January 2009, Hyundai reported a year-over-year sales increase of 14.3 percent. That compared with a 37.1 percent decline for the auto industry overall.

Realizing it was on the right track, Hyundai expanded on its innovation and launched Hyundai Assurance Plus to sweeten the deal. If the Hyundai buyer lost his or her job within a year of purchase, Hyundai promised to pay the loan or lease for ninety days while the owner looked for work. With this addition, Hyundai further bonded with its customers, making a clear "we've got your back" pitch to worried consumers. Bad news continued to buffet the auto industry that year, but Hyundai came through with far less damage than its competitors. While others were hammered, Hyundai just got dinged. A year later, company execs reported fewer than one hundred customers had returned their cars under the Hyundai Assurance Plan. But millions had seen the offer and identified with the car company that showed Americans it felt their pain.

This case study provides us with a clear-cut example of how and why to stay in touch with customers—not just as they move through the shopping experience with us but also as they move through their daily lives. By staying connected with its customers and listening with empathy, Hyundai was able to foster a conversation. In that conversation, it gathered real insights. When you understand the life your customer is living, you can create the products and services that customer would most appreciate.

Hyundai learned that its potential customers were so caught up in the everyday stress of navigating the economic crisis that car buying just wasn't a priority. When the brand responded by understanding and addressing their crisis mode, Hyundai immersed itself in the very real day-to-day experiences of its customers. That draped the brand in relevancy and set it apart from every other car—indeed, most other products—in the marketplace.

Harrah's: Using Customer Data to Create On-the-Spot Rewards

For our final case study, we will look more closely at the last word that describes this stage of brand ritual development: experiences. Often when we think of innovation, we think of physical objects: a bit of technology or other concrete manifestation of a new idea. But innovation is not just a product or service; it can also be an experience. We look now at Harrah's (which became Caesars Entertainment Corporation in 2010) because it is a brand that achieved success in this stage by focusing on delivering a terrific customer experience.

Harrah's was the classic story of a first mover lapped by ambitious competition. After opening its first casino in 1942, the company embraced physical growth as its success strategy. By 2000, Harrah's boasted twenty-one casinos in seventeen cities. It was a massive organization with a dizzying array of offerings and policies that had cropped up organically as the company expanded. It was a collection of fifty-plus years of ideas and projects cobbled together under one ownership umbrella. That's when newcomers to the industry began to explode on the scene with a glitzy array of must-see properties. With these new buildings came all manner of amazing attractions: the MGM had dolphins, the Mirage had tigers. By comparison, Harrah's properties looked old fashioned and unexciting. The new players were sucking up all the energy in the industry.

In an effort to understand its prospects for growth, Harrah's delved more deeply into its customers' habits. This revealed a stunning data point: for every gambling dollar spent by a Harrah's customer, only 36 cents was going to Harrah's. The rest went to competitors. The Harrah's customer was not cutting back so much as spreading his dollars across a variety of brands.

This is a classic scenario that plays out with every brand at some stage if it doesn't give customers good reasons to stick around.

Under the leadership of President and CEO Gary Loveman, Harrah's made a decision to compete for that full dollar, and a significant part of that strategy centered on the creation of better, more compelling customer experiences.

Harrah's became a leader in the collection of customer data. Its Total Rewards loyalty program allowed customers to collect points and use them across Harrah's properties. Total Rewards became widely used—as much as 80 percent of Harrah's revenues flowed through the program. This gave the company a perfect way to observe its customers and come up with new ways to improve their experience—thereby keeping more of that gambling dollar in the Harrah's family.

The first step was to use the banks of customer data to create what executives called a "dynamic and active customer service experience." A customer's habits, likes, and dislikes would all be collected and fashioned into a profile for that person. Employees would then have access to this information to create a seamless customer experience.

A loyal customer calling in for a reservation might hear: "Yes, it's our pleasure to serve you. Our manager says the first night is on us." A "Diamond–level" customer would be met separately, in a specially designated VIP room. A couple dining after a day at the black jack table would be presented at the end of the dinner with two free tickets to a show at a Harrah's property that night. All these efforts were designed to enhance the customer experience. Customers might have been used to receiving offers at home, via e-mail and direct mail, or over the phone. Now Harrah's was taking that offer process to the customer on the Harrah's property in a bid to improve their immediate experience.

Harrah's backed that program with new training for its employees, giving them tools and processes to do more than just be friendly to customers. They were trained and empowered to step up and make the customer experience better on the spot.

With these efforts, Harrah's was able to counter the "dazzle" factor of the newer properties. While they might be visually interesting and entertaining, Harrah's was able to make the case that it was the brand that knew the customer and was willing to reward loyalty with a great experience. Can a dolphin do that?

The Harrah's experience is one that shows how vital it is to resist the allure of chasing new customers. Had Harrah's followed the advice of the marketplace and poured millions into sprucing up its older properties and trucking in exotic flora and fauna, it might never have realized the gold mine it already had sitting in its customer databanks.

Time for Creativity and Vigilance

All these case studies show that this stage of the process is one where a higher level of creativity and effort is called for. Rather than relaxing— secure that your customer has joined your fold—you must be vigilant and step-up your efforts. It is not a question of giving your customer more promotions or more products. It's a time when you will have to offer something better and more innovative than you ever have before based on a clear understanding of their needs.

Your customer is at a unique place with your brand—almost at a crossroads. He might continue with you and embrace the brand as part of his everyday life experience, or he might decide he's traveled as far as he can with you and needs a change. This is the moment to make your case. And when you come up with innovative and relevant reasons, you seize the opportunity to seal the deal with your customer and move on to the fourth stage—achieving brand ritual status.

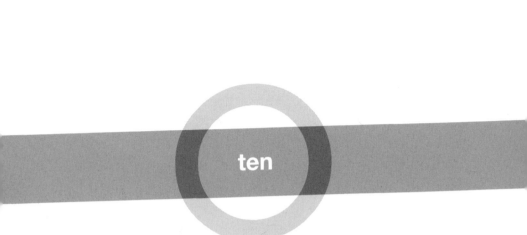

ten

Build a Bond by Aligning with Your Customer's Values

We've come to the final stretch of the process of building a brand ritual.

This is the stage where you have the potential for building a bonded relationship with your customer while enabling a new behavior in which your brand is the most essential component. I consider this the holy grail of all marketing efforts.

However, before you get there, you find yourself at the base of the summit. You got through the first three stages. You have a right to feel good:

- You convinced a consumer that he should try your brand. You got the first transaction by leveraging the New Value Equation.

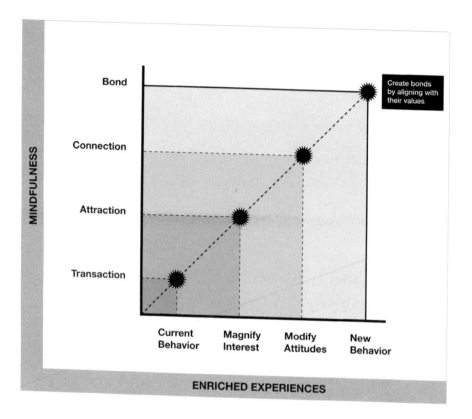

- Then you magnified your new customer's attraction to your brand by creating engaging experiences by using your brand's digital ethos.

- At stage three, you deepened the connection with your customer and modified his attitudes to make your brand meaningful in his daily behavior.

Now, in this final stage, you have the ability to establish a strong and sustainable bond. This is where your customer will go out of his way to choose you. He will insist on you when other options are offered, the way I do for my Starbucks venti every morning. It doesn't matter what city I am in: I have to find a Starbucks and get my venti Pike, double-cupped with room. Add four packets of sugar, some half-and-half and align the logos on the cup and the sleeve. With that, my day has officially begun. I won't do McDonald's or Caribou or Dunkin' Donuts. You get the idea. At this stage, I am the biggest fan of your brand—even without your bidding.

This state of a "brand-bonded relationship" is a very bankable stage. This is the stage of the deepest level of loyalty. Certainly, there is no chance a discount or promotion by a competitor will be enough to lure your customer away from your fold. When you reach this stage, a few cents off or a freebie is not going to make any impact. The switching cost for the customer, emotionally and behaviorally, has increased significantly. Your brand is not only emotionally connected but is also an integral part of their behaviors. This is the key. Once the brand becomes a part of the new behavior for the customer, it is very difficult for the customer to change this. This is the status we have been aiming for all along. You have the opportunity now to move to a *brand ritual*.

As we discussed earlier, the word ritual suggests that we are moving into new and hallowed territory for marketeers. Ritual is more than just habit or preference. It is an action infused with the most intense emotional fervor. It is almost religious in nature. When you get your customer to embrace your brand on a ritual level, you have created a very sustainable relationship. It is a state of bonding that transcends most marketing expectation, which makes it exactly what you should be aiming for.

Still, it is not an open door through which you can simply usher your customer. While connected to you, your customer isn't mindlessly locked in. This puts you at an interesting and critical juncture. Your customer might be fully satisfied with much of what you offer when it comes to product and service. But in order to move to ritual status—and even to maintain the connected status you've already achieved—there is yet one more field on which you must do battle. You must win at an emotional level.

Why is this important? In the world of brands today, there is a significant level of commoditization and homogenization. Most every brand in every category has the ability to deliver on the customer's needs adequately. They all provide the same features and attributes. They all are comparably priced. They are all conveniently available. Because of this parity, customers are looking for a different way to decide which brands they will allow into their lives. This is no longer a rational decision. It is an emotional one. The one way that they decide on the emotional quotient of brands is by looking at the brand's values and how they act within their ecosystem.

This customer interest in brand values is not a random development. It's part of a documented semiotics trend. Semiotics is the study of signs and symbols, and the discipline is a particularly relevant undercurrent of the customer/brand conversation. When you look closely at the semiotics trajectory on the emotional components of brand relationships, between the dominant and the emerging, you can begin to predict when and how a customer will look beyond your products and services to your brand values.

This is a complex and wide-ranging effort. Values that a brand espouses are not like an ad campaign or a new product feature. They cannot be turned on or off. They are not confined to a department or a silo. They have to exist across every aspect of your company, your products, and your presence. Everything you do has the potential to communicate your values to the world. This requires alignment across the entire organization and buy-in from the top.

Zappos: Happy Employees, Happy Customers

We talked about Zappos in chapter 7. Zappos is a company that grew up with values as a core part of its DNA. Early on, CEO Tony Hsieh made the connection between a happy corporate culture and powerful customer loyalty. He created ways to make employees happier: giving them more responsibility and control over their work and pay grades, offering clear paths to promotion, and consulting them frequently to keep them engaged and enthused about working for Zappos.

The company's devotion to its corporate culture is intense. Zappos sports a five-hundred-page "Culture Book" that not only lays out the values of the organization but also contains comments and testimonials from employees about what the culture means to them.

From this place of happiness, Zappos expects its employees to strive to make customers just as happy. The emphasis is on customer satisfaction. Employees are instructed to be humble, give "Wow!" service, and do what's necessary to please the customer.

Great customer service always helps to build loyalty, but the fact that Zappos looks to make its employees happy as well is another point of connection—one that is rooted in values. Just as a customer would prefer to buy a product that is not made in a sweatshop and to eat food that is grown in a sustainable environment, so, too, would today's customer prefer to buy from happy employees. When we as customers consider values as an important part of our buying decision, the relative happiness of the employee who serves us comes into play. We don't want to be made happy at someone else's expense. We want to spread the happiness around. Zappos makes clear that it does this every day. Customers respond by increasing their loyalty to the brand.

Today's consumers are very conscientious about the state of the world. They are living in a society of scarcity. They want brands and companies to care not only about profits and their business but also about things *they* care about. Like the environment. Like their communities. Like being fair to their employees.

Defining the Right Values

The key to infusing a brand with the right values is an important decision for most marketeers. We have all seen the damage done to a number of brands by "greenwashing" claims when the environment and being green was hot. Every brand felt compelled to be green, even if they really weren't doing anything meaningfully green. To find the right issue to support, there is an equation. It is a simple equation.

Brand Passion + Customer Passion = Aligned Values

You as a marketeer need to find the real issue that your customers care about, the one that they are most passionate about. Do they care about the environment? Are they concerned about their community? Do they want you to use fair labor? Do they want local products?

Then, you need to align this with the issue your brand can credibly support and the role it can fulfill in that category. For this to be real, your brand's passion for this issue needs to be based on the truth about your brand. It's dangerous to make it up. You need to ensure that the brand truly and genuinely cares about the issue and can take a stand for a period of time.

The world is full of things to care about, but this is the question for marketeers: what are the real issues your customers care about? You might think that a particular issue is critically important, but if your customers don't come to you with that same sense of passion, you will miss your mark. Customers don't want to be lectured about what is important in the world, least of all by their brands. What they want is to experience a sense of alignment with the brand.

Think back a moment to my ongoing use of the dating analogy. You have been dating an individual for a while and yet you are not sure whether you have met your "forever" partner. In a discussion one day, it comes to light that the two of you share a particular ideal or core moral value. Perhaps you share a deep religious view. Or maybe you both find the same philosopher inspiring. These are not casual connections but commonalities that make you believe this person is not just an acquaintance, or even a good friend, but a kindred spirit. When you find that individual, there is a thrill of discovery because it is a rare and marvelous experience.

This is the type of high-level connection your brand has the ability to make when you find the common set of values. When you as a marketeer are able to show a devotion to a value your customers already hold, that deepens the relationship between you—and communicates to customers on a higher level that they have made a good decision by selecting you. Not only do you provide a quality product or service, but you also are a good and right and just choice in the marketplace.

Discovering Shared Values that Matter

How do you find the issues that will resonate with your customers? In many cases, the best way to do this is to ask. Some of the most successful marketeers have been able to infuse their brands with a values-based bond by asking customers what matters most to them.

A great example of this comes in the backstory of the Livestrong brand. Much has been written about this brand and its success, but I want to point out a critical turning point in its evolution and elevation to a brand ritual. The Lance Armstrong Foundation was setting its agenda when it conducted a series of focus groups with cancer patients, survivors, and families. The information that came out of these conversations was illuminating. Foundation staffers had originally conceived of their mission as one of education: providing a place to share resources, studies, news for the cancer community. But when the focus group results came back, something else emerged: this community had a different goal in mind. It wanted a place to share stories, communicate with one another, and bond as individuals into a team of warriors—setting out to do battle with cancer on a variety of fronts.

Instead of fighting the news, the Lance Armstrong Foundation embraced this. It listened to what customers were saying. Then, in brilliant marketeer fashion, the foundation stepped up and focused its attentions on the values the customer was identifying. The foundation's work and communications strategy began to revolve around these priorities of story sharing and team building. By recognizing the values of its customer and aligning itself with those values, the foundation evolved into Livestrong and achieved fame and ritual status on the core strength of its values. But that information came to the foundation's attention only when it took the time to reach out and ask.

The message to the rest of us could not be clearer: *do not assume you know exactly what your customer is thinking.* Reach out and engage the customer in conversation. Take the time to do the research, review the information that comes back to you, and open your mind to what your customer is saying. The person who is already in your fold will likely tell you what you want to know—if you will take the time and resources to find out.

Discovering what your customers care about is the first step. To use that information effectively, you must also look within. What is a genuine and credible role for your brand? How can your brand live honestly within the values and issues your customers care about? This is an important intersection of your values and the customers' values and one that must make sense to customers in order to be useful to you.

Livestrong provides us with another instructive example along these lines. We've already seen the brand take the time to ask and understand the issues that are relevant to customers. Then the marketeers in charge of the Lance Armstrong Foundation took the next step and looked within: what genuine and credible role could the foundation play in this customer quest for story sharing and team building?

As it turned out, Lance Armstrong as an individual was a perfect fit for this set of values. A world-class athlete, he had already embodied the values of strength and perseverance in his many wins in the Tour de France and other elite cycling events. His success as an athlete gave him a credible place to speak about hard work, focus, and taking the long view. But the fact that Lance Armstrong was also a cancer survivor gave him another layer of credibility in this context. Any successful athlete could exhort cancer patients to be strong and stay focused on goals. Any could act as a motivational speaker and seek to inspire an audience. But as a cancer-surviving athlete, Armstrong could deliver this message with an additional punch—and that lent the foundation absolute authenticity. Because Lance Armstrong had lived the cancer journey, he could speak to the cancer community authentically because he knew their challenges from first-hand experience.

It is when the real issues of the community intersected with Lance Armstrong's genuine and credible status that brand ritual magic happened. Livestrong, which launched as little more than a website and a yellow wristband, became a phenomenon. It generated more than $50 million in 2009, and most of that from individuals who visited the site and wanted to be part of the brand. The alignment between brand and customer values was so strong, the brand name became a rallying cry, and Livestrong transcended its initial positioning as a brand by and for the cancer community to include the mass market. The match between values and brand was so perfect that everyone wanted to participate—even those for whom cancer was not an immediate experience. How many of us still wear the yellow band every day?

The important message for marketeers is that the Livestrong brand success was not an accident or an act of marketing luck. It was a rational execution, based on a clear understanding of customer values and the brand's genuine qualities. Through research and clear-eyed analysis, the marketeers of Livestrong created a brand ritual.

When the Values Conversation Breaks Down

This equation between customer passion and brand credibility is a critical element of success at this level. A miss on one of these can make the effort irrelevant. Look, for example, at an effort by Pepsi called Pepsi Refresh. In this program, Pepsi gave people the chance to get funding for philanthropic and charitable ideas. The program received a lot of positive attention for its digital execution, and many experts praised the program as smart way for Pepsi to maintain its youthful imagery and still push toward a new, more mature corporate identity.

All that said, Pepsi Refresh failed to push the brand into ritual status because it achieves only one of the key markers in this process of values alignment. Pepsi certainly made sure to understand what its customers care about. The realization that customers want a company the size of Pepsi to "give back" and support the community was spot-on. This is a mantra of many consumers who interact with mega brands. They want to see these brands do more than take their money. They want to see that money flow back into the community in positive and creative ways. So on that front, the Pepsi Refresh program was a fit: it aligned with issues that customers care about. It even went a step further and created a forum for customers to announce and publicize the issues they care about. This element of the program was well executed.

Where it fell short was in the second area—what is real and credible about the brand's role. What is credible about Pepsi as community change agent? Not much at all. The brand has no real status in this process. Pepsi has long been something you can buy in almost any store in every community, but few communities see or experience Pepsi as anything more than a consumer product. It has no credible status as a force for change or community improvement.

Look back for a moment at the Livestrong brand. When an athlete-hero-cancer survivor says "Livestrong!" the message has resonance. He has done that himself, and we believe him when he says we can do it, too. On the other hand, when Pepsi, a brand without a face, says "Refresh!" we don't feel that same values bond. There's little about Pepsi's history that makes it credible or genuine as a force for community philanthropy. As a result, this attempt to align a brand with values fell short. The Pepsi brand feels tacked on to the community-investment program. It could be any brand with a lot of money pushing this program. It's a good deed, to be sure, but not a program that puts Pepsi on the road to ritual status as a brand. The bond is not strengthened by this effort.

More and more, the creation of a strong bond is not optional. A brand might have success in forging a less emotional connection with the customer: one based on product, service, and price. But the values element is emerging as critical to retaining that customer over the long run. If it was once enough to provide a good product or service, today's customer has a more demanding expectation from brands.

The Rise of the Activist Consumer

From a cultural perspective, customers have come to see themselves as less passive and more proactive than ever before. In generations past, a customer might have felt powerless in the face of corporate stature; today that's hardly the case. Not only do customers feel they *can* influence the companies they patronize, they feel quite strongly that they *must*.

The vast majority of customers today believe they have a responsibility—not just an opportunity—to censure companies they believe are behaving in an unethical way. The rallying cry to boycott a particular brand because of its corporate behavior is a familiar one. Customers are well-used to being told to avoid certain fruits at the supermarket, shun a particular brand of athletic shoe, or refuse to buy a certain food brand because activists have made known that the company is not being a good corporate citizen. Many won't bother to wait for any organized campaign or instruction. When a catastrophic failure of a BP oil rig sent crude spilling into the ocean off Louisiana, customers stopped going to BP gas stations in the region, even though the oil company and gas stations are not owned by the same entity. Customers took it upon themselves to censure the brand for bad behavior.

The BP gas station boycott was not a stray example. Customers have evolved to be more concerned about a company's overall ethical behavior. It's not enough for a company to create a good product or service. It must also be a good company: good in a moral, ethical sense. A company has to stand for more than just making money. When customers go into a store or shop online for a product, they are more aware than past generations might have been about a company's conduct.

Many major brands have had to wrestle with this new awareness. Nike was already a giant in the athletic shoe industry when customers began to question its manufacturing processes. It was not the imperative Nike had imagined it would have. The company had come up in an era when its responsibility was just to make and deliver great athletic shoes. But as customers moved up the loyalty food chain and began to flirt with the brand ritual behavior, Nike found itself held to new standards—ethical and moral standards. It was not just a question of getting more loyalty from a customer. To keep its customers, to keep its status as a leader in the industry, it had to address issues that had little to do with footwear and everything to do with corporate responsibility.

Not only are companies expected to be socially responsible, customers increasingly want to see them lead the charge in social responsibility. They can no longer simply contribute money to causes. They must be leaders. Consumers today believe that businesses are just as responsible as government for driving positive social change. This is a shift from previous generations, when government was expected to carry the weight of social change and business took a secondary role. Today's customers want to see business step up. Those companies that do not risk the bond they have built with customers. A lack of social responsibility is reason enough for a customer to drop a brand—even a brand he has used for some time.

Marketeers need to view this greater attention to values not as a blip but as a trend. Customers are certainly taking the long view. Most believe the most successful and profitable businesses of the future will be the ones that practice responsible corporate behavior. Customers are certainly in positions to make that prophesy a reality.

As customer demands become clear, brands are stepping up into the values space with increasing effort and creativity.

In this next section, we'll look more closely at how some brands are moving their customers into ritual status by creating deep bonds by aligning with their values.

Whole Foods: A World of Stakeholders

Specialty grocers have been around for quite some time. So why did Whole Foods become a phenomenon? How did it go from regional player to the world's fastest-growing retailer? You can trace the company's trajectory back to its values: the ones management embraces and the way that the company communicates them to customers.

Whole Foods was founded on a core philosophy that puts its values out front and center: Whole Foods. Whole People. Whole Planet. That statement of values is key to its ability to elevate the relationship with its customers from simply loyal to fully devoted. Through its values, the company creates more than just a business relationship with the customer. It bonds with the customer in a mutual agreement on the role and responsibility of a brand in today's environment.

How are these values expressed? For one, the company describes its "stakeholders" as a broad spectrum of groups that interact with the Whole Foods brand. As CEO John Mackey said, "At Whole Foods, we measure our success by how much value we can create for all six of our most important stakeholders: customers, teams members (employees), investors, vendors, communities, and the environment . . . It is the function of company leadership to develop solutions that continually work for the common good."

This collection extends beyond the traditional definition of "stakeholders." Most companies would say stakeholder is another word for shareholder or investor. Others would expand the definition to include customers. A company hoping to adopt a more labor-friendly stance might add employees to that list. But Whole Foods goes another step by adding "communities" to its list of stakeholders, and still further by listing something as abstract as "the environment" as a stakeholder. This list is part of the values statement. It says to customers that Whole Foods is a brand that sees its mission as one that goes beyond the bottom line. By creating this long list of stakeholders, the company makes itself answerable on a wide variety of issues, from revenues to wages to recycling. It is a values statement that puts the company at the center of a full ecosystem of interests.

When you drill down into the Whole Foods business model, you see that ecosystem concept at work. With Whole Foods at the center, the circle around it has four critical points: team member happiness, satisfying and delighting customers, increased financial resources, and community and environmental responsibility. These points aren't arranged in a hierarchical list, but instead revolve around the core brand and coexist as equals. When a company places issues such as environmental responsibility on the same plane as financial results, or even customer satisfaction, that sends a message to the customer about the company's values. Individual customers who wish they could do more to help the planet are drawn to a brand like Whole Foods. It is a company that shares their values.

Marks and Spencer: A New Definition of Social Responsibility

Not all companies grew up understanding this connection between values and the creation of brand rituals. For some, the realization came in a period of adversity. This was the experience of Marks and Spencer.

The British retailer was already a household name but was losing ground to newcomers and trying to understand what had happened to its once-reliable bond of loyalty with shoppers. The firm was looking for a way to reenergize its relationship with consumers, and it found the way forward in social responsibility.

Customer research uncovered a shift in attitudes that led the way back to growth. At one point, about half of Marks and Spencer customers said knowing the company was a "responsible business" mattered to them. A few years later, that number was near 100 percent. The premium that customers were placing on values had skyrocketed. For many years, the company had engaged in what it saw as social responsibility through acts of philanthropy. But customers were looking for more, and unless Marks and Spencer was willing to align itself with the issues that mattered to them, customers would leave the company behind. Customers, management acknowledged, had raised their expectations of the brand.

The result was a shift in and expansion of the Marks and Spencer strategy. Rather than simply write a check, the company became more actively involved in creating more inclusive work environments, improving relationships with vendors, and communicating to customers that the brand understood its wider responsibilities to people, the community, and the environment.

The leadership of Marks and Spencer also made it a point to discuss how this renewed attention to social responsibility drove the company's bottom line. Its company chairman remarked on how the effort helped the company attract shoppers, recruit and retain top talent, form better partnerships with vendors, and create great value for shareholders. His observation makes clear that building bonds through values does more than create good will—it strengthens the business relationship and business performance.

Al Gore: Becoming the Voice for an Issue

Another example of values as a brand rescue strategy comes from former Vice President Al Gore. When Gore lost the presidential election to George W. Bush, he did so in a particularly brand-bruising way. It is one thing to lose because you did not get enough votes. But in the election of 2000, that's not what happened. The contest was marred by disputes over vote counts in Florida. The final blow was delivered by the U.S. Supreme Court. Gore did not lose in a dignified fight; he exited the stage sullied by acrimony and partisan sniping.

And yet that was not the end of Al Gore.

He roared back onto the political stage in 2006 with the film *An Inconvenient Truth*. It was a documentary based on a slideshow presentation Gore had been giving about global warming. It premiered at the Sundance Film Festival, was a critical and box office success, earning $49 million, and won two Oscars. Al was back. How had he accomplished this turnaround? He skillfully aligned himself with the concerns of the voting public. The increasing popular worry over global warming became his connection point. Gore, now also an outsider in the political process, placed himself as the voice of this rising unease. By aligning himself with the concerns of the viewing public, he was able to jumpstart his own brand image. He capped off his comeback with a Nobel Peace Prize.

Brand Ritual Is Everyone's Business

It's no surprise that this final phase of branding is the most complex to achieve. It is not attained through a moment of innovation in the R&D lab or a flash of inspiration in the marketing department. Instead, the status of brand ritual is one that requires certain key behaviors across the entire company. No single CEO can order this done. It can happen only through both that individual's leadership and the willingness of everyone in the company's ranks—from executives to sales reps—to follow.

Because it is so difficult to attain, brand ritual status stands apart as a true mark of distinction. Some brands, for reasons of legacy culture, might never achieve this state, no matter how good their product or service. Other firms will find and lose brand ritual status because they will be unable to hold the moral center that customers demand.

As customers, we were once satisfied to buy a good product for a good price. Today we want that goodness to extend beyond the confines of business transactions. We don't just want to *receive* good, we want to *do* good with our business. And for that to happen, our brands need to align themselves with our goals. The ones that do this are the ones we are willing to elevate from "favorite brand" to "brand ritual."

Afterword
ONLY THE BEGINNING

For years, I felt I was the only person in a room who looked at a brand—sometimes a ridiculously successful one—and began obsessing that something underneath was critically wrong.

I think it was a senior marketing executive in the audience at a conference in 2006 who finally helped me make sense of these uneasy feelings, even as he was voicing his own confusion about his company's relationship with its customers. "Zain," he said, "my brand is strong, but my business could be better. Is there something I'm missing?"

In a real sense, this book is a response to my feelings and that deceptively simple question. Here are some of the key ideas I hope you'll remember from what you've read:

- We are no longer in the business of creating images or attitudes and expecting consumers to follow us. It's not about consumer *beliefs*, it's about customer *behavior*.

- To be successful as marketeers, we must dump the marketing myths that don't serve us: that we can change customers' minds, assume the customer is interested, use advertising or social media as the key to branding building, and make acquiring new customers our top priority.

- We need to recognize and actually facilitate our customers' movement toward creating a brand ritual: 1) getting the initial transaction, 2) magnifying consumer attraction to our brands, 3) building connections with relevant experiences and innovations, and 4) creating a bond by aligning on key values. And we must do it in that order, without skipping or combining steps.

- Higher numbers of loyal customers are not only still possible but absolutely necessary if you and your company want to establish lasting brands that defy competitors for decades.

What's Next for Brand Marketeers?

Chances are, if you do a Google search for me, you'll find the description that I'm "one of the industry's best prognosticators." To reward you for getting this far in the book, I want to share my top seven marketing trends for the next few years to get you even more prepared to succeed in this business.

1. **Price commoditization will accelerate.** While consumers won't be looking for the lowest price (as they have in years past), what they define as a "competitive price" won't give companies much wiggle room. Pricing has become transparent. It's too easy for customers to check around to see what everyone else is charging for a product or service, so delivering differentiated value will be the key driver for success.

2. **Technology will continue to be the biggest driver of change.** This goes way beyond digital and social media. As with the pricing example above, technology genuinely

puts more power into your customers' hands. They will use it to be informed about, stay close to, and immediately respond (positively and negatively) to your brand. And you as a marketeer now have access to more tools to slice, dice, and analyze the data that customer responses are giving you. That means part of your job is to befriend your "inner geek" so you can listen to what they are saying, and then use this to better understand and manage your brand.

3. **Quality will remain important, but consumers won't pay more for it.** They expect that you will give them premium quality at that "competitive price" mentioned earlier. Consumers have moved away from that "disposable" phase and expect to keep products for a long time—emphasizing their growing desire for value and to protect the environment. Brands that can't provide this will see their share migrate to others that do.

4. **Digital won't take over the marketing world.** For years marketing industry Cassandras have warned that soon everyone will move all of their buying online, and stores and other channels are doomed. I love and use digital as much as the next person, but it's this forecast that's doomed. Consumers live in the real world. They want to interact with brands: to experience them in stores, for example. Winning marketeers will understand this and cultivate a multichannel approach for serving customers—and let the *customers* determine which channels are important.

5. **Society will see dramatic shifts in "old" and "young" behavior.** Young people will get older faster (in a metaphorical sense) because of all of the information that is coming at them and the speed with which this is happening.

The challenge for marketeers will be finding effective ways to reach increasingly discerning younger consumers to put them on the path to brand ritual status. On the other hand, older consumers will stay younger longer. You, too, might have heard that "fifty is the new thirty." Building brand rituals with them will require a deft touch, as they continue to demand the same premium quality and level of service at a competitive price and have the economic power to unseat a brand if their voices are not heard.

6. **Community power will increase.** Go back five thousand years to the marketplace in the Agora in Rome. Even then, there was someone who could tell you, "Go to *this* vendor. It has the freshest vegetables and the best prices. Avoid *that* vendor. The quality is not as good, and the prices are higher." Now we do this with digital communities. Just look at the impact of companies such as Groupon. All sorts of products and services will be developed that will leverage consumer power. As a marketeer, ensure your brand is capitalizing on this situation.

7. **There will be more "conscientious consumerism."** Brands that deliver value will only do part of the job. As a marketeer, you need to ensure your brand also aligns with consumers' values. In a world where products and services are increasingly homogenous and commoditized, your brand will need to find ways to set itself apart. Knowing what your customers value—transparency in your business model, being green, giving back to the local community, or other values—and showing how this is part of your corporate culture will help to build strong, sustainable brand rituals.

A Final Thought

Maybe you've heard it said or experienced it as I have: a person with average intelligence and a plan beats a genius with no plan every time. Now that you know why brand rituals are important, how they work, and have some of my ideas for creating them, what are you going to do?

My best counsel is don't stop now. Steep yourself in this idea. Hang out with "more knowledgeable others" by reading more books, blogs (mine is www.brandrituals.net), and articles on the topic and attending presentations, panels, and webinars. Enter the discussion— digitally and in person. When you're ready, share what you're learning with others at your company and begin to lead the dialogue there.

You read this book because you want to be more successful. As far as I'm concerned, marketeers have the option of creating brand rituals or watching their brands—and opportunities for advancement—get marginalized. Be the person who thrives in a challenging environment so I can read the book *you* write about it.

Recommended Reading/ Further Reading

Aaker, David. *Building Strong Brands*. New York: Free Press, 1995.

Aaker, David. *Managing Brand Equity*. New York: Free Press, 1991.

Baskin, Jonathan Salem. *Branding Only Works on Cattle*. New York: Business Plus, 2008.

Bedbury, Scott. *A New Brand World: Eight Principles for Achieving Brand Leadership in the 21st Century*. New York: Viking Penguin, 2002.

Humby, Clive, Terry Hunt, and Tim Phillips. *Scoring Points: How Tesco Continues to Win Customer Loyalty*. Philadelphia: Kogan Page US, 2003.

Jacobs, Ron, and Bob Stone. *Successful Direct Marketing Methods*. 8th ed. New York: McGraw-Hill, 2008.

Kitayama, Shinobu, and Dov Cohen, eds. *The Handbook of Cultural Psychology*. New York: Guilford Press, 2007.

Kotler, Philip. *Marketing Management*. 13th ed. Upper Saddle River, N.J.: Prentice Hall, 2008.

Lauterborn, Robert, Don Schultz, and Stanley Tannenbaum. *Integrated Marketing Communication.* Lincolnwood, Ill.: NTC Business Books, 1992.

Ogilvy, David. *Confessions of an Advertising Man.* New York: Atheneum, 1963.

Ogilvy, David. *Ogilvy on Advertising.* Toronto: John Wiley and Sons, 1983.

Reeves, Rosser. *Reality in Advertising.* New York: Alfred Knopf, 1961.

Ries, Al, and Jack Trout. *Positioning: The Battle for Your Mind.* New York: McGraw-Hill, 1981.

Scheuer, Jeffrey. *The Sound Bite Society: Television and the American Mind.* New York: Four Walls Eight Windows, 1999.

Acknowledgments

When I decided to write this book, I never imagined it would take a couple of years to complete. This is not a book of theory alone. It is a result of many years of my own learning, thinking, writing, and practicing the principles of building brands and growing businesses. It is also the result of significant contributions from colleagues, clients, friends, and family. I am fortunate to have these people, every one of them, share some of themselves with me so that I could gain from their perspectives and aggregate wisdom.

I have had the pleasure of working with a tremendous number of extremely talented people over the last couple of decades. To mention them all would take another book. I thank all of you from the bottom of my heart. You know who you are and how important you've been to my development as a credible marketeer.

I also wish to thank all my clients for their support, their patience, and their willingness to try new ways of competing in the evolving marketplace. To help grow your business has been rewarding.

Finally, I want to thank my family. Your support and patience as I put my thoughts on paper, sometimes over and over again, made a difficult task a lot easier.

About the Author

Zain Raj is the president and chief executive officer of SolutionSet, an integrated performance marketing company that represents some of the nation's most recognized brands. Zain leads nearly 700 employees across the national network of nine offices. His strategic approach and progressive solutions have resulted in dramatic top- and bottom-line growth for many companies in multiple categories. He has also developed proprietary intellectual property in the area of creating branded behavior change.

Before joining SolutionSet, Zain was North American CEO of Euro RSCG Discovery, the digital, CRM, data, and analytics arm of Euro RSCG Worldwide, as well as its Global Practice Leader for Retail Brands. He began his career at Grey Advertising in India before moving to the U.S. to join Wunderman Cato Johnson. Global leadership positions at Bayer Bess Vanderwarker, J. Walter Thompson and Foote Cone & Belding rounded out his management career.